THOUGHT
PROTECTION

THOUGHT PROTECTION

PARIS
TOSEN

Canada

Thought Protection is a work of nonfiction.

Second Edition, Reprint 2011

Originally published as *The Proper Protection of Human Thought* (2008) by Talessian El-Wikosian.

ISBN: 978-1-4611588-4-4

Book design and cover by Paris Tosen

Contents

PROLOGUE

A warning to the reader who expects to learn simple truths and well researched narratives; for it is fairly easy and cheap to find books that are well researched and written to entertain the reader's mind. But we must keep in memory that the reality we see with our eyes and the reality of spirit beings is part of the same reality.

When these spirit beings decide to share or teach a human being in the invisible world, they must send thoughts across the dimensions. Now if we accept the existence of multiple dimensions and therefore the existence of thought upon different dimensions, then, if something is visible in this reality then something is also visible in the spiritual world. Only our eyes cannot perceive it. Now the words of this book exist in multiple realities. The reader who comes to look no further than the definition of words is probably not fit to understand the mystical nature of this book.

A warning to the simple-minded reader who chooses to concentrate on the meaning of words. Far more important than the words is the message they carry together, and even more valuable is the meaning which is embodied in the words. A simple-minded reader will see words, an intellectual will get the message, a scholar understands meaning, the true essence of the book, and that meaning will be revealed over the course of time.

INTRODUCTION

What I will explain in the contents of this book will certainly cause you to think and rethink as to the validity of such information. This is expected and normal so it is written with this anticipation in purpose, but I will remind the reader that it is certainly up to you to decide whether you will adopt this knowledge and to what degree. That is the beauty of knowledge in general terms: it is available to your criticism or acceptance.

Ultimately, and in every single case, knowledge benefits you and only you. And in the macroscopic sense, the more or greater knowledge we have as individuals then adds to the amount and quality of knowledge we have as a collective, or, interconnected, whole. So it is in the group's interest that I present this arcane knowledge in the hopes that the technical details on human thought will necessarily improve and balance the current decrepit and unbalanced nature of this planet. It is obvious to me that the rampant spread of negativity, misery and antagonistic ideas through the mainstream news only supports my work's need here.

If, as a society, we need to search and scour for positivity and love, for what little traces of it we do find, then it seems to me that this situation is routinely unbalanced and in need of further examination. This is not to say, of course, that love and peace should become our primary activity because love and peace, although important, are just important components to a complex reality.

The reality we co-exist in is not composed on one particular platform, ie physicality; rather reality, as a concept, is set upon a multiple platform indivisible from all its parts but not all visible at all times. The visible portions of this reality is dependent upon the viewer, that is, in order to see certain things it is required that we be tuned in to certain frequencies.

This is no different in process to the workings of a television.

A television has no real intelligence on its own although it can process and translate electrical signals and then by retranslating those signals the television can stream video and audio messages. These messages differ according to channel, country and provider and, as well, due to nature of original message; whether it has been sent by cable wire, satellite or telephone wire or, now, perhaps internet.

So the television merely receives and decodes electrical data that is then presented as a sitcom or a news program. The content itself is prior recorded on tape or film, or live in some cases, and then broadcast via a specific frequency on a specific range of frequencies according to broadcaster and region.

According to the broadcaster we are limited to what types of information we receive since each broadcaster has specific content for a specific demographic. What is important to view here is the fact that the content provider allows the viewer to see only within the broadcaster's capacity.

You are hard-pressed to find serious news on a comedy channel or sex talk on a cooking channel. We have the option, depending on our television packages, to change channels, or, to change the frequency of our viewing.

If you recall from before, I mentioned that reality has many platforms and those are not always visible at all times. This is similar in structure, but not in practice, to television broadcasting.

Of course, we could also add radio and internet and satellite and so forth. Anything that operates at a specific frequency in a range of frequency, even military communications or short wave radio, operates on the same principles of television, and those all operate on the same principles of reality.

The question that will notably arise is how does one change the channel on the reality in question? Well, that would require several steps., The first step is to realize that multiple platforms exist. This first step is indeed a stumbling block for most people. Science has had a difficult time proving multiple realities in practice though it exists in theory, string theory comes to mind.

I am not here to profess or support any particular scientific theory simply because a theory in itself limits us. How? A theory tells us to validate its components, and if over time we do, then we are now limited to those components, ie we have a hard time to think outside of the theory if it conflicts with our main components. So, scientific theory is a good start, perhaps like religion, but it is only a good start.

The second step is to understand yourself. The purpose in understanding yourself is to understand what kind of "TV" you are, that is, what are you mechanisms for transmission and reception, and what are your processing capabilities.

The third step I'd like to mention has to do with accessing and activating your receptive capabilities. As most of you are aware of a repetitive life and repeated patterns within that life, or reality, you will come to understand that your access to your channel changer is severely restricted and atrophied.

So it is my own thinking that by understanding the foundation of reality broadcasting we will then be ready to understand the **malicious intention** ("malintent") that has strangled the public mind.

What you will learn in this book is not a theory and should never be treated as a theory. What is it? You will find here the technical underpinnings of the collective reality. There are individuals who fully understand these things and use it to gain power in the world; there are others who use it without understanding it; and there is the third who is befuddled. Then there are those who gain power and are befuddled.

The closest relativistic term we could compare to this technical knowledge is spirituality. But I want to make clear that this term, spirituality, has been largely misunderstood and under-represented in the modern society. Spirituality has to do with the spirit's connection to the whole spirit, the All and Everything.

The technical underpinnings of the collective reality has to do with mind, which is based in a denser and more malleable medium. Mind and its extremities is what is the focus of this technical book. Spirit will be dealt with another time for it is far more dense in complexity.

THE SLUMBER SOCIETY

The people of the modern world are sleepwalking. They are sleepwalking mostly without their knowledge or their realization; for if they knew and realized they would make a serious effort to wake up. This is why the idea of enlightenment or even epiphany is likened to a person waking up.

Over the course of spiritual recall, that is, remembering that you are a perfect and divine being from the start, you slowly follow a path of waking up. An awakened mind is a mind that has reconnected and accepted its divine nature.

The divine nature of a human body is the innate nature of a human being. This innate nature is called "divine" simply out of historical reference, but divinity is a misunderstood term in the developed society. Divinity, because of its association to organized religion, is often feared in actual fact. It is

9

feared because people fear that being divine will make them easy to control and brainwash by the religious fundamentalists. But let us be clear that to be divine is quite the opposite of control, in fact to be divine is to be free of control, any kind of control.

So each human being is a divine being and this divine characteristic is an innate characteristic, that is, divinity is not earned, divinity is recognized. It is recognized through the acceptance of this innate fact. The acceptance of this innate fact will achieve enlightenment. So that is the only challenge; actually two challenges, the first challenge is to remember that you are already a divine being. The second challenge is to accept that as truth.

It is the case today in the world that humans have been disconnected from their divine self; and this disconnection prevents them from achieving an awakened mind.

This disconnection, as we experience in our disconnectedness without other members of society such as marriage trouble, relationship instability and vile behaviour, is unnatural.

It is unnatural because it is within the capacity of your human experience to connect to your divinity, and that the better the connection the better your relationships, the better your marriage, the more isolated the corrupt and the greater moral contemplations that will take place in society as a whole. A subtly connected society, connected to its innate divinity, is non-violent and compassionate.

Obviously the case today is a tremendous tendency toward violence, corruption and division; therefore, there is a *disconnectedness* in the world and this disconnection is unnatural. When a divine being, such as yourself, has been disconnected you become zombie-like. You begin to sleepwalk without knowing that you are sleepwalking. You being to feel angry without knowing why you are angry. You begin to feel empty without knowing why your life is meaningless.

You see, the minds of society are in tremendous pain as they attempt to resist the cover takeover of their mind's operating systems, as they are hijacked by unscrupulous, that is nasty, people who belong to elite pockets of wealthy societies. The elitists are an unempathetic and egotistical bunch obsessed with the acquisition of power, control and all the benefits of such material things. And these elitists are very determined to maintain the status quo, that is complete control, and are continually tightening their grip on our minds.

The more of society that attempts to wake up from its slumber through spiritual contemplation, activism and meditation, for example, the more extreme measure these elitists take.

We must remember that there are many ways to maintain control, whether these methods are visible or not. For example, the collapse of the World Trade Center in New York on September 11, 2001 was not designed to kill people in the name of any religion, rather the collapse of the building and the loss of life was a symbolic shock designed to **hijack** your mental, emotional and spiritual states.

Even after four years many people have yet to fully recover and during those four years the elitists have further tightened their grip on your mind without your knowledge. These elitists will stop at nothing to accomplish their goals.

In order to make all of this more pleasant I suppose would be to introduce a new line of pyjama since everyone, essentially, is *sleeping*. This would change the fashion sense for certain. Of course, it is important to maintain a sense of humour during these trying times since everything is temporary in nature and since you now have access to a process by which you can remove the malicious intent and other negative intention that have been downloaded into your system. Malicious intent is one of the ways in which your mind may become hijacked.

This is due partly to the advance of electronic technology, particularly communications technology, and partly due to excessive population growth. Technology is combined with media – TV, radio, print, web, mobile – to infect the greatest number of minds with the greatest possible effects.

These elitists have become not only elusive but efficient and people, you and me, have been lulled into a prison of comfort; a prison with rules and a system that demands our allegiance.

If indeed you are on the path to enlightenment, as indeed you are because you are reading this book, then the only way to begin the process of waking up under the continual bombardment of suppression is to reconnect with your divine self.

In order to find your divine self, your spirit or true self, you need to remove all the malicious intent in your mind, heart and soul.

The process of clearing away malicious intent, especially after many years of infection, is not an easy task and will require your utmost diligence. You may find it useful to work through this process with a trusted friend or perhaps a group of like-minded individuals. The amount of time it will take depends on your ability to deal with the accumulation of lies that your life is based on and your ability to accept the greater truths that make up this reality.

Your success will also depend on your ability to prevent further infection from malicious intense since these negative intentions are being continually spread by the elitists and their hijacked cronies. You see, not only a small percentage of the world are bent on control but they have in their employment, through their elusive hijacked means, a large number of people. These people are scientists, teachers political leaders and plumbers; these people are celebrities and CEOs. Malicious intent is widespread and once a mind has been infected it then follows the exclusive agenda of elitists.

This world is facing a systemic hijacking. And just like a computer virus, or spyware, infects your computer and the network of computers, malicious intent is destroying humanity one inch at a time, one neuron a minute, one good idea a second, one code per nanoparcel.

Maintaining a positive attitude and trying to be happy are like using dishwashing soap to clean up Chernobyl. Do not buy into these elitist-inspired lies. Disinformation is one of the techniques of malicious intent.

If you are still in need of proof in order to believe my own thoughts then I only ask you to observe the situation of the world; environmental damage, pollution, violence, absence of morality, inability to love, obsession about money, prevalence of war and the focus on celebrity and looking beautiful. These are the facts of life. You are part of these facts. You are sleepwalking among these facts. The fact that you are sleepwalking means that you are infected with malicious intent, and having me try to prove beyond the obvious is futile. The proof is all around you. Accept that, and all things improve that much faster. So, it is first about acceptance, oui or non?

The fact that you are reading this book means that you are searching for a way to cleanse yourself. This book may not complete the process but this book will certainly get you started. This book will empower you and give you the ability to make clearer decisions about who you are, what you stand for and will help you to connect with your true self. What you do from there is your choice. So that's the purpose of this book, to enable free choice.

Of course, if you believe that you already chose what you do with your life then I'd only recommend replacing your current wardrobe with a full pyjama collection. If you're going to sleepwalk why not dress for it. The old adage, dress for success can now be "fashion for slumber." *(my term)*

The truth is we are not free in the real sense of the word. The concept of freedom that has been disseminated to the public is false, it is another form of malicious intent. If you buy into their sense of freedom you surrender your mind and you become susceptible to being hijacked.

Real freedom, if it should be known, is not found in a political or religious ideology. Real freedom is not earned; Real freedom is not fought for, these are forms of misinformation. Real freedom is remembering your divine self and accepting that as a true statement. There no need for battle or discussion because it exists externally. It is in front of you now. You only need to clear the path.

Thought Protection

You cannot see it because the unnatural obstructions surrounding you, draining you of your spiritual self. You are feeding the energy vampires who hide in the shadows and only appear when it furthers their aims. Do not buy into this, reconnect to your true self and you will wake from your slumber and when you awake you will never fall asleep again. The choice is yours. The choice has always been yours. Only now you have some tools to help you.

Remove the malicious intent and other negative intentions and set yourself free. Wake up and see the world for what it truly is. Only when you are awake will you be free, and the elite vampires will fall out of power and they will be exposed. And the world will become an advanced society in every sense of the world.

THE NONCONFORMIST MIND

Heresy is an opinion in philosophy, science or politics that does not conform to the current administration of accepted opinion. The word 'heresy' comes from Greek to mean, *choice of beliefs*, that is, the beliefs that oppose the standard thought, or, the orthodox position. One can stray to the left or right of the central orthodox position. When you lean away from orthodoxy you deviate and are a *deviant*.

Heretic priests, in the yearly years of history, were excommunicated, ie banished, until they admitted their guilt and asked for forgiveness. Later the Church began the Inquisition to suppress heresy and this is where the burning at the stake took place. Heretics, also called *dissidents*, held unorthodox views such as the belief that the universe is vast and filled with inhabited worlds.

Thought Protection

The purpose of the Inquisition, through the Catholic Church, as to defend its beliefs and to condemn those who spread false doctrines. Copernicus and Galileo were two great thinkers who were condemned and banished by the Roman Church because their theories were contrary to the understanding of the Scriptures.

Heresy has not disappeared, neither has the Inquisition, and continues on in what is known as conspiracy. What is conspiracy? It is an agreement between two or more individuals to plot against someone or something in the future. A conspiracy theory is a way to explain a situation as a secret plot with a covert group of players. Whereas the admission of guilt in the heresy years could grant you forgiveness from the Church, the admission of guilt today offers no such luxury. Conspiracy theorists, whether right or wrong, are largely discredited, some mysteriously die, and the weapon used against them is to convince you that the orthodox position is the supreme and pure standard. That weapon is malicious intent.

The years have passed on and the methods have changed but the terrain is the same. One cannot transcend the corruption of the minds of society without dealing with the mechanism of a mass hijacking. I suppose then that the process of change begins here by exposing the fundamental structure of a metaphysical tactic. The metaphysical tactic is designed to root out any deviation from the authorities of thought and to redirect human thinking onto the standardized and accepted modes of rationality.

Yes, certainly you can deviate and if you do you will be branded as a nonconformist and generally will not be accepted into mainstream society. You may already be this kind of person, a person who doesn't fully identify with the mainstream, a nonconformist. You may have even developed your ideas and skills and earned the label of a *radical*.

We cannot be certain that you are 100% right or 100% wrong. That isn't even the point of this book. The point of this book is that regardless of who or what you are, it is important to remove the toxic and negative intentions that have flooded your system, and by doing so you will gain better access to your true self, be it you call it your divine self or spirit or soul or god.

WHEN YOU DEVIATE FROM THE ORTHODOX VIEW AND BECOME A NONCONFORMIST you are already more connected to your true self than with those who maintain status quo as a hypnotized public.

A radical is both dangerous and liberating at the same time. They are dangerous because they may be filled with disinformation and are taking action on disinformation. Again, disinformation is information that is both factual and false. If I said, for example, that a car is too expensive for the average person I would be misleading you. Why? Because cars come in different price ranges and have different financing options available. Plus, the idea of the average person is not defined. What does that mean?

So a radical (and a radical can also be a person in position of power) believes that breast cancer is on the rise. The radical believes that because a 'trusted' source told them that. Obviously that statement "breast cancer is on the rise" is not necessarily true, only that it has been broadcast into the public.

The radical, taking this as important, begins to believe that they must change their diet and lifestyle in order to prevent breast cancer.

Our radical in this case is a woman, if you haven't guessed. The radical, always preoccupied with the threat of cancer, modifies her life in order to be healthy and free of disease, but the woman doesn't realize one important thing – the possibility of breast cancer and the fact that it is on the rise has entered her pattern of thinking. Thought becomes reality.

The ironic part of all of this is that breast cancer only rises because of paying more attention to it, because if it is agreed that breast cancer is on the rise then breast cancer will rise. With higher breast cancer rates more people are convinced, we can see how things might get out of hand and how drug companies can find room for profit; for if you wish to adjust your profits you only need to adjust the public perception. (Bird flu is another *scenario* but the public resisted enough not to allow this to get out of hand. With bird flu we can see how the public's resistance to malicious intent can prevent disaster.)

The radical, bent on a healthy life, finds a malignant lump in her breast. How did that happen? How is it possible that such a healthy person could get such a horrible disease? Well, if you understand malicious intent you will understand that the statement "Breast cancer is on the rise" was broadcast as a piece of helpful information on the surface but really beneath that it had a negative intention that influenced your own subconscious mind into allowing the disease to take root.

We could spend endless pages of identifying statements and information and having deep discussions about what was the intent of those things, but I think that method is not productive. That method exhausts energy and distracts us from the primary function which is to cleanse out all malicious intent.

The authorities would have us spend our energies proving things and doing in-depth studies with error variances and meanings of interpretation. Now perhaps that can be seen as outside my primary abilities by some, or, perhaps that can be seen as a way to distract us from the truth. The truth is always found within yourself and the cleaner you are of malicious intent and the other negative intentions the better able you are to identify and process the truth. We have all seen scientific studies that prove coffee, for example, to be good for and coffee to be bad for you.

Well, what does that mean that coffee is good for you and bad for you? That is disinformation. What does it mean when they say that war is wrong and war in the name of freedom is just? Which one is it? Disinformation? What does it mean when they admit that ETs exist and that they are evil? Disinformation. It is the example a friend of mine used where she said it's like giving us a cake with rat poison. Would you eat a cake? Yes. Would you eat rat poison? No. But what if you didn't know there was rat poison inside the cake?

A theory comes along that says a bunch of elitists have expertly and covertly hijacked the minds of society and certainly that theory is categorized as a conspiracy theory. But let's back up a little bit and review that is going on again: a few elitists have joined together to covertly control the human population and are using malicious intent as one of their weapons. It sounds to me like these elitists are the ones who are conspiring. It seems to me that they are part of the conspiracy. But we'll never prove it they think. Because they have infected enough minds that even if the truth were told tomorrow the public would find it hard to believe, not to mention the fact that if the truth were told a strategic campaign of disinformation (malicious intent) would confuse or overburden or cause forgetfulness in the population. So this then has been the historical case and why they continue largely unimpeded.

Thought Protection

It is the same as if a large congregation of starcrafts showed up over every major city in the world. The elitists have already branded star beings (ETs) as evil and as enemies so would we really be willing to shake their hands? Certainly not. Well, not in large numbers anyway. In fact, most people brainwashed to believe the ETs as enemies would join the human military as they strike against the friendly star beings who certainly have not shown us to be evil or violent.

As you can imagine then this current psychological situation is difficult to navigate. It is purposely difficult to navigate so as to protect those in power. What is right? What is wrong?

Do not spend your time on these things; instead, FOCUS ON THE REMOVAL OF MALICIOUS INTENT.

Research, study and discuss things as you see fit but do not obsess over it for it will distract you and make you vulnerable to further attack. A computer that is infected with a virus or spyware only become more infected each day that it is not cleaned until such time that the computer crashes and no longer starts, and if your data isn't too corrupt, or deleted, then your computer may be saved. If not you can buy a new computer. But if your mind crashes once too many times it may leave you catatonic and in an institution with a free set of pyjamas.

If the real world situation is any indication then many minds have been damaged. There is evidence for this. We can look at the rate of depression, insomnia, hyperactivity, bipolar condition, anxiety attacks, stress and so on. Lifestyle and job stress do not cause these conditions. In fact, many of these conditions have no known cause. Doctors cannot identify the cause of depression and neither can they tell you how drugs to treat depression work and yet millions of people take antidepression pills.

Pain relievers, pain killers and tranquilizers are very widespread, especially in the developed world (The underdeveloped world is too busy with civil war, disease and basic food). How much pain is society really experiencing? Is it just good advertising on the part of companies or is it something else?

The real conspiracy is not coming from the mainstream public. The real conspiracy is coming from an elite group with capable hands who use *spreaders* to spread malicious intent as hackers use viruses against computers.

These malicious people and their malicious weapons are hard to trace. In fact they are so well hidden by now that it would consume all your energy to find them, not to mention in trying to bring them to justice. They could be anybody really. They need not look weird or be of any particular age. That is why I always recommend adhering to the principle of the simple path. Cleanse yourself routinely of malicious intent and use caution and common sense when acquiring information.

The following chapters will become both more esoteric and technical in nature. Since we are dealing with a complex metaphysical system, that is, a biological body converging into a spiritual (nonbiological) core connected to some kind of electromagnetic grid, we must be able to balance both logic and imagination. As you can see then we must be able to use both sides of our brain in order to comprehend and maximize the use of this information. As I've said before, and I'll say again, we need diligence, discipline and determination with no expected outcome.

The only thing we can rely on is a thing known as possibility. The world we live in is a world of possibility, which means that no matter your current situation it can be changed.

All things are possible at all times. The progenitor of that possibility is hidden in the complexities of your mind, and your thoughts. This also makes you realize that the mind itself, a part of consciousness, exists on multiple levels.

These multiple levels, since it is dealing with consciousness, are not visible to the human eyes (although this is not entirely true). What does that mean? It means that you will be working with, perhaps, unfamiliar sensory organs as you navigate these different realities.

It means that what was once comfortable may become uncomfortable and what was once familiar may become unfamiliar. These things are necessary. These skills will also benefit you in other ways over the course of your life experiences. I bid you a safe and enlightening voyage.

THE HUMAN SYSTEM

In light of the fantastical information put forth and the metaphysical nature of a human being, I'd like now to discuss the human system. The human system is poorly understood as a complete system because of the division between science and spirituality. Science in general, be it biology or psychology, understands many details of the mechanics of the human body. In fact, it could be said that the human body has been mostly defined, dissected and detailed to such an extent that the only further details science will discover is in the higher ranges of the electromagnetic spectrum, magnetic resonance imaging (MRI) comes to mind, but, most people are familiar with X-rays.

The human body, the biological hardware, with physical parts and components is so well understood that transplants, for example a heart transplant, are becoming quite common. Science, it can be said, has indeed advanced to a very high level including genetic manipulation and tissue growth.

Spirituality, mostly on the basis of religions texts and authority, understands many of the unexplainable processes of the human spirit., Unfortunately, there is no common consensus as to the exact spiritual nature of the human being, that is, mystics agree that a spirit, or, soul, exists but it has neither been measured, detailed or dissected in the scientific sense.

What does this mean? Well, the human being's better half, the spirit, is largely undefined. The human spirit, the existential software and a nonbiological construct, is very poorly understood because religions per se have, not only failed to evolve, but failed to advance. Religion is so backward; in fact, that worshippers are continually searching for the traditional orthodox methods of daily worship, since they believe that traditional is equivalent to pure truth. This is simply untrue.

So this is where we are: we understand body and do not understand spirit. We understand the hardware and do not understand the software. And this is how a human system and a computer system differ. This is the only reason why a computer system is perceived to be superior, or smarter, and a human system is perceived to be inferior, or stupid. These perceptions are based on a false and incomplete understanding of the human system.

Computer software, for example, comes in many varieties used to provide many different kinds of applications. A software application enables you to accomplish some task, whether it be word processing or instant messaging. There are reliable software applications and unreliable ones. The difference between the two is how negatively they affect the base operations of your computer, as well as how often those applications crash. We all have experienced a crashed computer to some degree. A crash occurs when the operating system can no longer process the application, that is software, and becomes overwhelmed.

As a non-expert in computer systems, I feel safe in discussing the general attributes of a function or process, the details of which you can research on your own peril. Computers crash regularly. This is a result of the interaction between the software, the hardware and the operating system.

The reason why an operating system is important for our discussion is because the operating system found your home computer can be equated, for the point of our discussion, with the human mind. The mind, of course, completes the basic attributes of the human system: body, spirit, mind, and those three areas are all interconnected in more ways than we can understand.

For purposes of this book, we are dealing with the mind, the operating system or a metaphysical being. The human mind is far more resilient and capable than any artificial operating system, because the human mind is part of an infinite network of intelligence and energy. The only way that a human mind becomes reduced in its operational efficiency is when the mind's connection gets impaired or cut off from the *metaphysical network*.

The metaphysical network permeates every aspect of existence and is the basis of all things. Call it the Matrix or God is regardless of what it is, and what it is can best be described as Truth. Truth, obviously, is an esoteric term that is hard to understand as one person's truth is another person's lies. But that is the nature of truth, isn't it? Truth is based on a personal and private perspective, assuming of course that we have not been misled, or brainwashed to see different.

Thought Protection

You see, the mind is pliable, not just with your own intent but also by outside intent. This is similar to a computer virus attacking your home computer. Most computer viruses attack the operating system. Spyware, on the other hand, attacks your internet browser.

The internet browser is also part of mind. The browser, for short, can navigate the terrain of the internet, or the worldwide web. Notice that the 3-Ws of the worldwide web do look like the waves of an ocean.

This is not a coincidence and neither was the fact that Netscape Navigator or Internet Explorer were given those nautical titles. The internet can be likened to an ocean with points, or destinations, of information, pleasures and ideas.

The matrix of our metaphysical reality is no different. We can, as well, navigate the seas with our minds using our intention as our propulsion and our thoughts as our compass. Then you can see that the mind is hijacked can be redirected to unfamiliar waters or held captive in dangerous terrain.

Many seamen and ship captains feared the presence of pirates in the old days of the seas and high adventure. Pirates could steal your gold, kill or take your men, or, worse, could hijack and take over your ship. Well, today, just as is the case for computer systems, the human system can be hijacked and taken over. This hijacking can be both on purpose and by accident, as you shall see.

Make clear the similarities between computers and humans, but always understand that the human system is superior in every way and that the only way a human system becomes inferior, and stupid, is when a human mind is hijacked and their thoughts are redirected.

The day that science and spirituality do meet, like the current cooperation between hardware manufacturers and software programmers, will be a day when we will be better able to integrate body and spirit, as well as mind. Currently, these three systems are divided. There are reasons for this certainty. Certainly if a human being had full access to infinite knowledge and truth then it would be harder to spread lies.

You can quickly check up on facts on killer bees, for example, by way of the internet. Facts in hand you can hold your own during a discussion about killer bees. But what if you didn't have internet access nor a library card? What would you do if someone told you that killer bees had invaded your hometown? You'd run inside and lock the door.

Now if you had internet access you'd find out that someone was exaggerating to make you scared. There's the old adage that knowledge is power. It is not that knowledge is power, but, rather knowledge enables clarity and clarity leads to good decisions. Decisions in and themselves are powerful. Taking away, or modifying, someone's decisions are also powerful.

What connects knowledge and decision is a thing known as **thought**. And now it becomes clearer, you see, if you can covertly redirect thought you can necessarily alter decisions. I think this needs repeating: THE REDIRECTION OF THOUGHT ALTERS DECISIONS. Thought is controlled or guided by knowledge so, therefore, control knowledge and you control thought and decision.

How do we acquire knowledge? By using the mind. Hijack the mind, the ship, and the navigation is no longer congruent with truth, that is, your ship is no longer your ship.

We have to be clear that your mind belongs to you, that is, unless you don't want it. That's a whole different story and always by choice. But I'd recommend keeping ownership of your ship, you'll be pleased to discover your true self and your life's purpose, whatever that may be.

And I suppose that is what this is all about, isn't it? It's about truth, whatever that means. Life is about discovering your truth in order to partake in a truthful existence.

If you have never known your truth, your true nature, then you may be the victim of malicious intent.

You may also be on the other end of the spectrum, one who always knows what to do only to find out years later that it wasn't what you wanted after all. And the point of all is that life is a challenge and it is meant to be a challenge, but *malicious intent* can destroy your life purpose and block you from knowing what is in your inherent right to know.

The key rests in understanding body, spirit and mind. The mind connects us to truth, or knowledge, and truth enables good decisions. Truth also enables us to learn about spirit and this is helpful since spirit is poorly, at least incompletely, understood. It is not the focus of this book to explore spirit. Mainly, here we are focused on mind and the basic metaphysical stage upon which we are asked to act. It is a wonderful stage. It is a glorious life. There are no correct words that can fully express the beauty of this reality once we awaken and see this reality in all its splendour.

It is unfortunate that many minds of society have been unlawfully hijacked by purpose. It is an unfortunate situation, but not a hopeless situation. The human mind is very resilient and has access to an infinite intelligence network; therefore mental freedom is always available. You only need to realize that truth; you realize that truth by waking up which is achieved by clearing your mind.

THE MODALITY OF THOUGHT

Therefore we are able to reflect because we are not only mirror images but we are mirrors. Like looking in a mirror.

In order to change the appearance/ image reflected in mirror we need to change the self. If we see hair growth on our face then to remove that we shave. If we shave then the image is also clean shaven.

Now if the image is your physical body in the material reality then where is the other self that creates this image? There must exist another body. This other body influences the material body. Therefore, to cause sadness (ie depression) we inspire sadness in the other body which is immediately felt in the material body.

Thought Protection

Obviously this other body is invisible to the native human eye, just like your mirror image cannot see you. The other thing that is invisible is thought. We can tune our thoughts like the tuning dial on the radio to broadcast information or to receive information. We can also block information, change the volume, and turn off our thoughts.

If the radio analogy is true then it must also be true that there must exist a technology that enables this thought processes, that is, a technology that can reflect the different modalities of thought.

The technology must be able to both receive information (data, knowledge, facts, ideas) and to transmit information. This receiver-transceiver works at a very subtle level and is within our ability to control, that is, this technology is owned by each individual.

A popular technology that modulates and demodulates and commonly found in mobile phones and computers is known as a *modem*. But a modem is of a material nature and is an actual component. To me, this modem has escaped our detection because it is obvious to us, for one, and, for two, we are clouded by scientific necessities.

The only logical place to find a modem that works with the modalities of thought and the complexities of mind is the white and gray matter located by your bone skull. I'm talking now about the brain.

We use no more than 20% of our brain because we have been prevented from understanding the last 80%. You will not find the mathematical proofs here to support this claim/theory because I am not a mathematician.

Using the logic I have set forth we can plainly see, and necessarily agree, that if thoughts are invisible, but exist and if our material body is a reflection of an invisible body then the technology to connect these two things needs to exist. And if we are dealing with modulation of thought and demodulation of thought then we are also dealing with some kind of modem technology. Our mobile phones have built-in modems and yet how many people are aware of this? How many people know what a modem does? How many people know what a brain does?

Well, if we use a generous 20% of our brain then even the brightest mind, a genius, cannot fully understand the complexities of the human brain because even a genius is limited to using only 20%

of their gifted brain. Now all of this is true unless we understand this, either implicitly or explicitly, then those individuals have been able to exercise the untapped applications of the human brain. They are only exceptional because they have spent effort to develop this technology and to apply it. But each and every human being has the same biomolecular apparatus, though some individuals have problematic modems, such as the case with retardation and certain cases of mental illness.

If the brain is a modem, and from a logical viewpoint there is no other apparatus in the body that is so widely misunderstood, then it must be able to comprehend the different vibrational frequencies that circulate the grid of earth. I prefer to use the term navigate since the sea of information is very fluid, almost like a liquid mirror, or, a fluidic mirror.

So, the mind itself then is the ship and the brain is the modem. But since the physical brain must operate on some physical principle, such as your limbs are mechanical to some extent, then the logical possibility is that the brain operates using electromagnetism.

Electromagnetic energy includes all the things we can see and cannot see, for example, microwaves are unseen and yet exist. A mobile phone receives a signal from a cellular tower and yet if we look at our mobile phone we cannot see those waves of energy. Neither can we see thoughts but we can feel them. So the modem can receive thoughts, invisible, and then transforms them into feelings, physical. The feelings are physical because we now know that the Other Body reflects emotions to our physical body. So this modem is both biomolecular and electromagnetic, or, perhaps, we can just look at it as a biomagnetic apparatus, or component.

I prefer magnetism in this regard because magnetism is far more subtle and, therefore complex in nature and is the basis upon which earth exists, while electricity per se is still largely a human construct. Also, electromagnetism, or light, and thoughts are different, that is, light affects another area of the human bodies and that leads us into things of a spiritual nature, that is why focusing on magnetism we can remain focused on thoughts and not be distracted by divine things which are far more idealistic and evasive, and even, dare I say controversial.

Thought Protection

I don't mind controversy since controversy is a human necessity, that is, the ability to argue enables learning and understanding. Any mind who accepts things is a hijacked mind, and a hijacked mind is no better than a shoe on someone's foot.

So magnetism and its spectrum of influence must be the spectrum of thought influence, that is, the extent and purpose of the modality of thought exists, and operates, on a *magnetic vibration*. This magnetic vibration is very subtle, very persuasive and very potent.

In fact, thought modulation shapes the very nature of reality and that is why if thoughts are redirected then society is redirected.

The way to redirect human thought is to hijack the mind, either individually or collectively. This, as I understand, is a critical situation in the world today.

Human thoughts have been modified and redirected in a very perverse and unnatural way and that is now reflected in the state of the world.

So here again we find ourselves with a very obvious piece of evidence, that is, the existence of violence and hatred, the threat of war, the prevalence of fear, the lack of love and compassion, the continuance of disease, the growth of mental illness, all these things and more are a reflection of misdirected thoughts, whether acknowledged or not. You do not need to be aware of your hijacked mind to have a hijacked mind. In fact, since most of what we discuss here is unseen then it seems obvious to me that the process of hijacking is very difficult to trace, and only skilled mentalists can such things be known, or, even understood.

Even as I write these words I am aware of the complex nature of these things. Perhaps in the scheme of things I am not the most competent to explore all the facets of thought modification, but that has never been my strength. My strength is to bring to focus unseen possibilities, to bring to the surface that which we fail to see so that we may see and understand.

The things, the knowledge I am revealing here is poorly understood by even the greatest scientific minds because of the many reasons; the most prominent is that the left and right brain hemispheres are still divided, and knowledge is gained when they are merged. Yes, science understands brain processes, plasticity, memory function and storage, some neurochemical striations, and even mind control through programming, but my discussion is on **thought redirection** on a large scale.

Now the modality of thought has been lost to us for many many years, and what we are seeing now is that this modality of thought still exists, has always existed and will always exist. The only thing that changes is the extent in which we understand this innate gift each individual has access to. It is a gift for a person to have ownership of their thoughts and therefore ownership of their minds which is important to the navigation of the sea of information.

Mind ownership, as also a captain to ship, is essential in order to pursue the things we wish to pursue, be it your purpose or your mission, whatever that may be. Your life experience is entirely related to the direction of your navigation and wouldn't it be empowering to have mastery over the navigational controls?

We mustn't let ourselves be redirected to dangerous waters. We can, if we choose, be redirected to unfamiliar waters, we can be guided to many wonderful places, that is always an option. What we must be wary of is how malicious intent redirects human thought. Again, intent in and of itself is necessary to protect ourselves from that intent which is malicious and negative.

Intent can almost be compared to software. Using software is vital to enjoying the inherent power in a computer but malicious software, spyware and viruses, can damage or cripple your computer and kill your data, or can hijack your system for unlawful purposes.

Learn to regulate your thoughts. The experiences of your life and the very nature of your being are dependent and shaped by **intent**.

This is just like your computer system is dependent of software. The computer software enables an application whether it is a game or word processing.

The application enables an experience and produces some kind of result. Intent is no different in its application. Intent enables an experience and produces some kind of result.

The result of an intent, or intention, is best understood as a manifestation. For example, if because of fear you think that no one will ever love you then the result is that no one will ever love you.

Thought Protection

The negative intention produces exactly what is demanded. If your intention is to make a certain amount of money then you are likely to make a certain amount of money. Many self-help books have discussed these ideas and I don't intend to labour over these things. (Intention and living your purpose or destiny can conflict because, for example, if we wish for lots of money but your purpose is to walk a spiritual path then you will not receive that money, unless perhaps you first walk that spiritual path. Intention always follows your role here on earth.)

What I simply wish to remind you of is the fact that intention is the enabler in the reflective process. Intention is reflected from the Other Body to the Mirror Body. If intention is the software then thought is the code. So by reprogramming the code we change the software; by redirected thought we change the intent.

By changing the software, intent, we change the experience. Therefore, by hijacking the mind and redirecting thought we effectively change the course of life, and, on a large-scale, that of human existence. We can call that a mass hijacking. We can call it mind control. We can call it belief. We can call it democracy. We can call it ideology. We can call it whatever we like but the bottom line is that we are dealing with intent. We are dealing with thought modification. We are dealing with a power that we are only starting to understand.

That power is vital to our human existence whether you believe that life is an illusion, a dream, a nightmare, a hell, a fantasy land, or what have you. We own our thoughts, or codes, and we determine the kind of intention, or software, that is available to us. Sure, some of this is affected by your destiny, if you believe that, and your heritage, if you are aware of that, as well as your own disposition and purpose. Those things are better left to you to reflect upon since they directly benefit you and are best understood by you. No one can tell you who you are. Only you can determine this.

Knowing who you are is a process and evolves over your cycles of growth. All of this is connected and shaped by your level of readiness. Only when you are ready will you be able to understand things. When you understand things then you will wake to new things. When you understand you will see things differently, your perception will become clearer. The clouds of doubt will fall away and you will see who you are.

Thought Protection

Learning about who you are, your true self, begins with clearing your mind of malicious intent and other negative intention. Only when the captain has returned to the ship's controls can the ship be properly navigated. Be the captain that you are. Be mindful. Be free of maliciousness.

THE MULTIPLATFORM WORLD

Being that we exist in a complex reality and being that we perceive multiple realities within that reality which we think to be singular and complete when in fact it isn't – we are struck with an outright situation of conflict and confusion. Let me use the dream as an example to help us understand the concept of perception.

There is no individual in this reality who does not or has not experienced the dream concept, that is, has experienced as shift in consciousness while in a sleep-like state. The shift in consciousness has also resulted in a shift in perception and enabled the individual to visit and experience the construct in a different reality.

Thought Protection

The dream construct, in its simplest form, in a very real paradigm with a very real purpose, as we shall see. Using the dream as a paradigm we can better understand that beyond this physical and dense reality that we see, hear and touch there exists another reality by way of a paradigm shift during the sleep state which enables us to transcend reality of matter and to exist consciously in the reality of imagination.

The dream concept has existed since the beginning of all things that contain consciousness because those things which contain consciousness also contain spirit and spirit is part of the great spirit, the All, the Source. The dream concept in its basic form is a second platform to this whole, complex reality. The first platform being the material world.

The imaginary world then is a second platform based on a different set of scientific and spiritual roles, that is, what is applicable on the first platform may not be applicable on the second platform. For example, you may use a mobile phone to contact your mother in the first platform but your mother may be represented as a female deer (doe) in the second platform and that may be the extent of your communication. While the first platform (reality) uses the clarity of words and the nuances of expression and social custom within the confines of technology and distance, the second platform (imagination) relies on symbols, telepathy and non-local awareness among others.

The imaginary world, as a conceptual and constructive tool, is limitless, that is, the imaginary world is limited by the individual. It seems to me then that by limiting the individual's sense of imagination we would severely cut them off from the true power of their imagination. I think this has largely been the case with the technocratic leaders who have instilled upon the collective group of individuals, better known as society, the idea that you can only believe truth that which is proven in science and technically approved by rigid examination. Trust that which is proven and if un-provable, as is the case with imagination, then do not trust, these are the beliefs downloaded to society.

These beliefs are false beliefs. To see truth only in one platform is to disconnect from Source and to allow yourself to be manipulated by the technocratic leaders. You see, technocracy is the next level of government. It is to be, if properly installed, the last level of government because in order for technocracy to govern the great majority of this world's individuals will have surrendered their imagination and will have been completely severed from Source.

This does raise a pertinent question and that is: What exactly is Source or the All? I believe that this is a very relevant and important question since we are now crossing the realm of religious talk. I do not believe that this is a religious talk. Neither is this a spirit talk. This is merely talk. This is merely a discussion of the way this complex world is structured because if we understand the structure of the world then we will understand our transitory place in the world and we can understand how to maximize the full benefits of our experience.

Again, the idea of both religion and spirituality are man-made ideas as are the ideas of good and evil. The only benefit to constructing evil is to profess goodness. That way when those things labelled evil, be it an individual, a group or an idea, are attacked and destroyed it will have been done in the name of good. But the decision on what is good is a deeply prejudiced label. This has been a large problem in the material world that has been able, across different leaders, to condemn certain individuals or cults or theories as evil in order to prevent the erosion of their power and control over society. It has also enabled those in power to destroy, cripple or cleanse that unlawfully named enemy. But the naming of the enemy is largely arbitrary and completely dependent on the agenda of those in need of power.

What is good and what is evil? Who is good and who is evil? Are you evil? Of course not. No person would ever claim to be evil unless they intended to remove those who claimed to be good. In that case it amounts to the same situation as good wanting to slay evil. The division and labelling are human constructs.

Religion and spirituality are human constructs. Though they may have been inspired by holy texts or personal experiences the labels themselves are man-made, that is, artificial. Anything that is invented by human beings is artificial. This is not to say that it is good or bad, it is only to say that it is unnatural.

Nature, as in the case of a tree for example, does not understand the difference between religion and spirituality. If a spiritual person chops down the tree or a religious person chops down the tree, doesn't matter. What matters is that a person chopped down the tree. The bottom line is that the tree was chopped down.

How does all of this relate to the multiplatform world? In a very imperfect way, the way in which are perceived things is largely labelled for us, by this we can refer to the real world and the dream world. As you can see we have effectively labelled, in an artificial manner, two of our platforms. We have labelled them to differentiate them from each other.

We could say, for the sake of argument, Platform A and Platform B. Platform A has denser characteristics as Platform B which is based on more imaginative characteristics. I think that the process of labelling is not inherently improper unless it is divisive or competitive in nature such as good and evil.

In fact, at this time, I do not see a way out of this labelling process although I think the label should be more truthful to the situation, for example, instead of the dream platform we could say the imaginative platform and instead of the real platform (real world) then we could say the conscious aspect of the human brain which is in fact very small of humanity in general as we shall learn.

So this is where we are: the first platform is based on conscious thought and is called the Conscious Platform and the next platform is based on the imagination and therefore will call it the Imagination Platform. We'll use these terms, at least temporarily, so as to better understand the multiplatform world.

I think over our understanding we will come to use better terms, perhaps. I do not know if it is actually necessary to use the better term. I think a term that clearly helps us to understand or to better explore each platform is the better term, that said, there is no ultimate term per se, and these will evolve over time as our understanding of them improves.

This now brings us to the next platform. If we primarily exist in the conscious platform and access the Imagination Platform in our sleep then we have probably covered the majority of the platforms that we would expect to find.

And yet this is not the case. The Imagination Platform (dream state) has been used to rationalize what goes on when we sleep in order to control us in the Conscious Platform (waking state).

Thought Protection

Most people do not recall the details of their dreams, as well, most people do not recall the details of their past actions. This has to do with the existence of a factor called forgetfulness. Memory loss is very prevalent on the Conscious Platform. This is an unnatural thing. Memory recall is important in understanding the multiplatform world.

The process of memory as an existential process the way in which humanity is able to connect the verifiable dots within their patterned lives through the process of memory we piece together information and thereby improve our understanding of ourselves. Through the process of the memory we can also reach the higher platforms in the world.

Memory is eroded through the use of chemicals and pollutants, seen and unseen, over a period of time. The rise in dementia and Alzheimer's is evidence that we are being slowly lulled into a hypnotic state of compliance.

Compliance is reached with memory loss and forgetfulness. If we forget who and what we are then we can be reminded through psychological reinforcement who we are not, and we can be reminded who are our false, self-elected leaders.

So here we have a problem and clearly one of the reasons why we have trouble reaching the next platform. Also, when memory is repeatedly blocked or redirected it is then we form habits that actually take physiological and neurological precedence over our material being.

I will explore these concepts later on, for now I'd like to continue with the multiplatform structure. The third platform can be reached during the basic mental state known as meditation and its rapid entrance into the mainstream via yoga and alternative thought is enough to convince us that meditation is the gateway into the third platform, and that society is striving to gain access to higher platforms, despite actions taken to prevent them from doing so. This is also to say that the fact that the mainstream has learned meditation only suggest and confirms that there are indeed higher platforms that are being used to control and manipulate society for the purpose of control and power.

The meditative state, along with the waking state and the dream state, is reached by allowing the conscious mind to relax and the unconscious mind, the spirit, to overtake the process of perception. In meditation, or, the Meditation Platform, we are able to lay with *astral* ideas, to retrieve certain information and to also cleanse out polluted thoughts or energies. In fact, when the conscious mind is relaxed we are able to experience the flavour of our divine, that is, unlimited nature.

Not only that but in the Meditation Platform we can improve ourselves, stabilize our conscious self and feel that we are loved despite otherwise. In this Third Platform we can balance and understand ourselves better.

The Third Platform (meditation) is reached by calming our conscious mind of the daily distractions, of which there are many, and by allowing our unconscious mind, our spirit body, to pass through the conscious barrier, the mental firewall, and to literally exist as a separate part of your physical body. Meditation (or reflection) as a practice is only hard because of the daily distractions we are unnaturally subjected to and allow ourselves to be subjected to.

This now brings us to the next or Fourth Platform. The method used is *thought management*. The thought realm, like the meditative, dream and real, is considered to be the Intention Platform.

Unlike the previous three platforms, the Intention Platform is reached by a process of intention. Now the process of intention is a very obscure process simply because at the scientific and technical level there is minimal support and there aren't many experiencers (available) on this subject. This was also the case with meditation but personal experience on a large scale has changed all that.

It is common now to have meditation retreats in the mountains and on exclusive islands and so forth. Intention is not an easy thing to grasp with our conscious mind, this is why we must rely on our hearts, or the energy from our hearts rather than the mental energy from our brains. This alone is difficult for people since their heart energy has been polluted with fear, anger and hatred over many years so the process of intention cannot be fully achieved until the heart is cleansed.

The First Four Platforms

A shift in consciousness and perception enables an individual to experience an alternate reality. Some people can do so consciously, some unconsciously, some with assistance and others by circumstance. Each reality platform has its own texture and protocols, that is, the navigation through them is unique and we are unable to exclusively rely on the tools of the other platforms. (The first platform is densest, most physical.)

First Platform
Conscious Platform
(realworld)

Second Platform
Imagination Platform
(dreamworld)

Third Platform
Meditation Platform
(astralworld)

Fourth Platform
Intention Platform
(thoughtworld)

It is not within the scope of this book to assist in cleansing the heart energy. But I do think that by understanding how malicious intent can redirect human thought will certainly help you to identify, locate and remove those things which block your pure access to heart energy, or to achieving and using the power of intention, the Intention Platform.

This, by the way, is the platform that is largely, not exclusively being used to control human thought.

As you can see then this book will spend considerable time on the Fourth Platform (intention) since this is the platform where we can regain our elusive sense of self, and that is the ultimate aim of this book: to regain your thoughts so as you can make decisions with clarity, honesty and responsibility.

As this will require the bulk of our work, I shall leave the remainder of the platforms for another time. Now, we must move on to the next topic and this has to do with self-understanding.

THE SELF AS A SYSTEM

We have so far established the existence of the multiplatform world. The multiplatform world so far includes the *Conscious Platform, Imagination Platform, Meditation Platform* and *Intention Platform*. Although there exist a greater number of platforms in the reality complex for the scope and purpose of this book we will concentrate our thoughts on the first four platforms since it is in this realm that the majority of human thought is redirected.

I will try as best I can to refrain from using the words 'manipulate' or 'manipulation' since these words infer that you can resist and this doesn't seem to be the case. What I will show is that our entire system of thought cannot be manipulated, rather it is redirected and in its new focus gains access to unreliable, wrong, or misleading information and knowledge. And that is the major problem in society today.

The redirection of thoughts through unlawful and highly technical means using the metaphysical medium, that is, the spectrum of communication that remains invisible to the eyes and impacts the realm of the heart.

Each platform can be understood to act as its own network of information with its own network protocols. This is quite similar in function to a local area network (LAN) or another wide area network (WAN) in computers. For example, the intelligence agencies use a highly secure network with proprietary information and knowledge that requires a user to log in and be monitored as part of a larger organization.

The intelligence network is only accessible by an intelligence agent or operative or higher level user. This contrasts sharply with say a library network which catalogues millions of books and research papers over a period of time, and is accessible by those in possession of a library card or school card, without prejudice or qualification, that is, anyone can get a library card and can keep a library card unless they accumulate excess and unpaid late fees;

otherwise, a library in its construction is available to all.

If we compare the intelligence agency with the library we find ourselves unable to compare them, that is, their structure and purpose and technical design are widely different.

It is important to understand that difference because the same can be applied to the multiplatforms. The multiplatforms, although far more esoteric and abundant in construction, are similar to these area networks in operation in universities, government, corporation, military and so forth. When a system of knowledge is large enough and important enough, a technical network, a *platform*, is set up. So then we can also understand these networks as platforms. The internet is another platform, only a more public platform.

If we look at any platform closely we find a number of options or gateways to explicit knowledge. These are typically tabs or topics that are clickable. By clicking on one of these tabs we can enter further into a topic and explore further details of information. Every platform then has multiple gateways, call them entry points or doorways, or, simply topics.

A platform, it must be understood, is not a gateway: A platform is a closed area network of knowledge, ideas, information, experience and shared co-existence. A gateway exists within a platform and its purpose is to enable the gathering and accumulation of specific data and details regarding your personal need and desires. There is no judgment here as to your purpose for entering a gateway within a platform, in other words, you are free to use that knowledge as you will. That is the structure, or really unstructure, or free will. If you can access the platform, eg the Meditation Platform also known as Unconscious State, then you are free to navigate its contents according to your skill.

The platforms are inherently multifaceted and symbolic and it is not that they are constructed as multifaceted and symbolic, rather a platform, especially the higher platforms, are structured by the users, that means you (the higher you). The symbolism and multifaceted expression is your specific mindprint as a result of your own emanation and desire. In other words, the higher platforms are very fluid, or ethereal, in nature and it is why only certain minds and competencies can navigate the higher platforms. A competent mind is not easily achieved and without proper conditioning, a mind can be damaged by trying to access certain platforms prematurely.

Be warned of this in advance. Be warned that the world we perceive either by vision or thought is very complex and very elusive and one can get easily lost in a platform and may never find their way out.

It is my own thought that some problems in society such as dementia and certain mental illnesses, eg schizophrenia, is due to a mind's accidental access to a higher level platform and by that mind's inability to successfully navigate its contents nor process the advanced knowledge gleaned or downloaded. Whether by accident, or on purpose, we can reach a platform. Psychedelics, mind altering drugs and medicines, are and have been commonly used to reach an altered state in order to gain access to a different, presumably higher, platform. So have meditation and dreaming. All tools.

That access, without navigation skills, can be detrimental to an individual's mind which may not be apparent until much later in life. Traditionally, psychedelics, whether herbal or pharmaceutical or both, have been used under the guidance of a teacher, be it a shaman, a mentor, a book, or a spirit being. This was done to ensure that the individual's mind was not damaged in the navigation and that what needed to be understood was understood. These kinds of experiences are done in a limited basis for the average person who is clearly unprepared on the most basic levels.

Accessing the Meditation Platform via projection is relatively safe, but even so having a meditation teacher can help you to navigate the platform and to gain knowledge and understanding, or, better known as wisdom. Wisdom is the obtainment of the whole puzzle, that is, the piecing together of all of the separate parts; the understanding that everything you did was done for a reason of which finally has become clear.

It should be apparent now that the platforms can be navigated as if they were oceans and your mind was a ship. In any ocean or sea there are various water conditions and numerous dangers. An experienced captain is able to navigate treacherous waters and perhaps even avoid pirates or submerged icebergs.

You are a captain in the multiplatfrom world and you must learn to navigate the seas of knowledge. Your ship is your mind. It is the only ship you have so you must protect it; for if it becomes damaged it is difficult and slow to repair.

So this is the situation: a multiplatform world and six billion ships (since there are that many people on the planet at this time, not including other lifeforms like trees, animals, insects, spirit beings), or, six billion minds. Some ships may be larger, faster and better equipped than your ship.

Some ships could act as battleships with an intent and purpose to destroy other vessels, or, at least to damage them. Some ships, or, minds, may be lost at sea or crippled in the ocean of knowledge. There may be pirates who steal knowledge from your ship for their own purpose, good or bad.

As on the high seas there may be many events or experiences that may be found. What I will discuss here is the act of hijacking since I believe that hijacking is a very innocuous and untraceable thing.

Your mind, ship, may be easily hijacked by unscrupulous people and processes. In fact, it is extremely likely that your mind has already been hijacked and is why you are reading this book.

It is common these days to feel that there is something wrong in the world, whether at work or at home or with the geopolitical situation, and it is this feeling that should suggest to you that your mind, to some extent, has been hijacked, that is, your thoughts have been redirected.

What does it mean to have your thoughts redirected? It means that the information and knowledge you are receiving is untrue and unreliable and ill-suited to your life and purpose. It means that you are brainwashed. It means that you are anchored to an information source that does not properly and completely resonate with your true self.

Brainwashing is an outdated term and most people don't believe that they can be brainwashed because they believe that they are in control and that they make their own decision. But this is the power of hijacking at work because unless you are aware of the acts of hijacking then you are not aware that it has occurred. We must consider that hijacking is not necessarily bad or obvious. In fact, as I have said, hijacking is a very innocuous thing. For example, you find yourself studying business administration at university after being inspired by the CEO of a pharmaceutical organization.

Thought Protection

Your 'inspiration' leads you to go to business school with all the fire and determination and school loans that you can muster. But, it is possible, especially when you learn of some of the illicit processes of the pharmaceutical business, that your mind, was redirected to study business, but really wanted, say philosophy. It is hard to know for certain what you wanted to study, only you know that. Sometimes a hijacking can be positive, for example, redirecting an alcoholic to sobriety.

Let us be certain that hijackings are commonplace in the world, on the multiplatform world (look at advertising which is strategic thought redirection for market access). Where we run into problems is the owners of information, content, media because it is these owners who then limit our learnings or focus because they feed us their content and we, with few options, are forced to set sail on a dangerous ocean. The fact that the world is in a miserable state, that disease is rampant and that war continues is only evidence of this.

So we must be vigilant in our quest to maintain control of our ship and navigate the seas of our choice for the right reasons. The right reason is found with the proper purpose and is discovered with a good compass be it the belief in god, or spirit beings (offplanet cultures) or simply in the belief of "doing good" in a misguided world. Since at the heart of the matter, there is no good or evil, only misguided souls.

THE MORTAL LANDSCAPE

After establishing the existence of a mental ship in a sea of knowledge among a number of platforms of experiential learning we inevitably arrive at a complex area of differentiation, that is, we have thus far assumed that in the realm of thought that we are free. In fact, the idea of the freedom to think is probably one of the most misunderstood areas of the modern world.

It is obvious that if you look in a mirror that your mind, contained within the complexity of a biological brain and a neurological system, is unbound. Your thoughts are owned by you. You think and make decisions according to your own desires and needs. These desires, needs, wants originate from you though may be stimulated by various forms of propaganda (eg Suffering from depressive thoughts? Try our brand new drug that is recommended by 8 out of 7 specialists who we never paid "directly" to support our claims and to downplay the list of side effects including pelvic fribulations, hippocampus arthritis and muscle wonks).

Regardless of how you are influenced to buy certain consumer goods or how much personal insurance to buy your thoughts, that is, your beliefs, convictions and invariably your wisdom is your own. But this is where there is error. You see your collective beliefs are not yours. They have been leased to you by a mind owner.

The collective mind, as if a piece of real estate, is primarily owned by others, mind owners, and these mind owners manage the property and own the rights to this property, and you merely lease or buy but never truly own. In fact, if we continue with the real estate analogy we can understand that the land belongs to no one since it is part of the planet.

So this is the mental landscape. An ethereal landscape managed by mind owners and widely sold, leased or rented to individuals. So this is the situation. The situation is that what you believe and invariably think is not owned by you though is within your power to cultivate. This is no different from a home/land owner who cultivates a garden and plants various flowers and trees over time.

A home/land owner can also decide, according to their level of wealth, what kind of home to build or buy and what color to paint the exterior. And, of course, the decoration and design of the interior is done at their leisure and whim. Once the title of the land, mind, is settled then that land (mind) owner is "free" to develop their lot. But we must remember that the division and distribution of land is an arbitrary distinction because the land belongs to no individual or corporation; instead, belongs to nature, to the planet, and to the collective reality. There is no ownership.

The land ownership analogy is useful to help us understand mind ownership. Let us be clear at the outset, and as you have seen so far in this exploratory book, that you have en-masse sold, borrowed, leased, bought, rented the current space of your individual thoughts, beliefs, and attitudes. This is worth repeating: your current allotment of thought is managed by an outside agency. How can this be true?

Admittedly this is difficult to accept or understand, and most certainly that would be the case. The idea that an outside agency owns the rights to your beliefs, thoughts and attitudes is certainly a strange and outright fantastical idea. Again, if we look at the current state of the world we are reminded that the level of violence and disease far outweigh the level of love and compassion. They are not even balanced.

It is important to understand this concept of mind ownership, or, at least to accept to the fact of its validity before we continue because it is imperative to understand, and this is why we explore the aspect of truth, that reality at the conscious, imagination, meditation and intention platforms is managed and monitored by various outside agencies both with self interest and with loving compassion.

This is the mindscape then, that the lower the platform the less obvious this truth becomes, that is, in the denser consciousness platform we are blind to see thought and intention, only we see the result of thought and intention. If you wish for money you will have money or a rich lifestyle. You believe that your actions and hard work enabled you to reach your level of wealth. You believe that your sacrifices made it all possible.

Thought Protection

The true case is that you engaged to strive for wealth so that other individuals could get more wealthy and so that a nation's economy could become more powerful. You justified this by believing that wealth is good and that you were satisfied with the level of your comforts. These beliefs did not originate from your true self, rather they originated from the mind owners who had it in their interest to propagate wealth in order for them to become wealthier and to ultimately maintain societal control.

The mind owners are very proficient at managing thoughts and beliefs, and to most people the idea of someone, an outside agency, controlling their beliefs is absurd. It is only absurd because they have been lulled to believe that scientific explanation and theoretical basis along with a good dose of proof is required in order to substantiate a claim.

People in general have been lulled away, or hijacked, from correct thought. What is correct thought? Correct thought is the process of thinking that is free of restriction. Scientific proof is a restriction. Logic, on the other hand, is a tool to enable thought because logic stimulates the rational process, and rationality, we know, is part of the human mental operating system.

Paris Tosen

Rationality seems to be part of reason and reason is one of the key differentiation, and mysteries, that separate mankind from the animal kingdom. Reason is a kind of mental software that is also malleable. Give a person a good reason and they will accomplish anything. Give a person a bad reason and they will not even move. We are propelled by substantial reasons to do substantial things. Reason is the way that mankind is collectively inspired.

We could spend considerable time on reason and still not fully grasp the idea, that is because reason is the process of our thoughts that is easily hijacked. At any one time our reasoning is not fully under our control even though it seems this is the case.

For example, a person may reason that a diet soda, that is a soda with an artificial sweetener, is a better choice for them because they are several pounds, or more, overweight. This is a fairly common thought built on the reason that weight concern can be managed by non-caloric. But where did this reason come from? Certainly not from the individual.

The reason to use an artificial sweetener was download from an advertisement or transferred from a trusted friend, or similar reason. Certainly the reason did not originate from the individual although that individual may believe that it was their choice. And this is the problem in modern society: It is easy to believe that the choices we make originate from us when in fact this is not necessarily the case.

In case of the artificial sweetener the lack of calories, the protection of their physical appearance, does not equal the disease-causing nature of the sweetener. A cigarette smoker feels better with a cigarette and yet the cigarette is actually proven to cause cancer and illness. Although a cigarette smoker may claim problems with addiction, I would argue that there is a greater problem with reason. Their reason has been hijacked. We all have our reasons for doing things. We chase wealth. We strive for self-improvement. We are eager to marry and reproduce. We kill those we label as enemies. We backstab our competitors. We remember to hate. We compete for everything.

We cheat and steal if we won't get caught. We have our reasons for doing so, and yet, if we examine this process (more closely) we discover that our reasons have been hijacked. And this is the central theme of this unusual book. What we believe, and our rationality for doing so, is not as completely in our control that it seems to be.

THE MAGNETIC VOYAGE

All materials are influenced by presence of magnetic
field.
Arise from movement of electrical charge.
Magnetic field contains energy.
Magnets used in radio antennas.
Plastic magnets.

If magnetism is involved in thought reception and
since magnetism surrounds earth planet and if
human aura surrounds body also magnetic, ie
attraction and repulsion, then we can also attract
and repel thought, ideas, knowledge and so on, that
also says that a thought has a magnetic field around
it.

Earth has field, body has field, thought from body
from earth must also have field. So this is what we
are missing. Thought is magnetic energy, not
electrical. Electrical assumes speed and motion and

therefore time and distance, but thought is instantaneous; therefore, magnetism must be the instantaneous field since earth operates under magnetic force.

If earth body has a magnetic field then human body must necessarily have magnetic field; therefore, if brain is part of body then brain also has a magnetic field. It would be logical then, by extension, that the mind, being a part of the brain aspect also has a magnetic field, but we know that the mind is like a ship; therefore, the ship must navigate a magnetic sea. So from this we can understand that the mind is floating on a *magnetic substance.*

The magnetic substance is abundant only because it needs to support or accommodate billions of minds, as we see them as ships. Now since these neurological ships can presumably travel at limitless speeds we can understand that minds per se equally limitless, that is, *intention as an engine,* is limitless.

The intention engine's propulsion system has a number of controls and the most likely of candidates for these are: confidence, conviction, congruency, compassion, and conditioning. By adjusting these controls, we can adjust the propulsion system. Now malicious intent then has the ability to hijack the engine control room.

With the engine control room hijacked, or, no longer under your command, the captain has little choice but to surrender to the demands of the pirates. Who is the captain?

Well, what is a captain? A captain is one who determines the ship's voyage. A captain understands the ship, its strengths and weaknesses, and a captain commands the crew. A captain must also understand the terrain, map, and the inherent possibilities, or likely dangers. Pirates are one of the dangers that come with any voyage.

What is the difficult issue is that the hijackers are *noncorporeal*, that is, invisible. The ship is also invisible as is the sea. When we speak of being invisible we speak of things that the naked eye cannot recognize. We don't recognize a soul yet a soul exists. We don't recognize love yet love exists. We don't recognize a mind yet mind exists. Many things exist despite whether we recognize them or not.

We also cannot recognize magnetism yet magnetism exists. And it is upon a magnetic sea that the human mind sails. And upon this unlimited sea, a mind may encounter many dangers and many opportunities.

As well, it is possible that a mind, a defenseless mind can become attacked by negative intention. The negative intention, causing damage to the invisible ship, can, over time, cause a ship to sink, or, to breakdown.

We have seen this and labelled this as a nervous breakdown. But prior to the sinking of a ship into hopelessness and despair the mind will likely experience panic attacks, depression, mood shifts and so forth. In other words there are signs of damage and signs that the mind is under attack from negative intent.

So we have established that there exists a magnetic sea upon which the mind is free to travel. The sea like all seas is fraught with danger and opportunity.

As the captain of your emotional crew, you can use intention to propel you toward your course, or voyage. And the direction you choose depends on the thoughts you make since thought is like the compass.

As you can plainly notice we have invariably found ourselves on a new kind of terrain, and this terrain is vitally important to our mission here on earth.

The magnetic sea is unlike anything we have yet to discover and yet we have traveled this sea for many years. We own these minds and these minds, as ethereal ships, travel from point to point and port to port. Our thoughts direct us in the best direction, using the safest and most efficient routes, at least those routes known to the captain. This is why an experienced captain knows which ports are worthless and which ports are worthwhile. We call this person wise and this person is golden with age.

Perhaps then the captain of this ship is what we have come to know as the soul. An old soul, that which has lived many successful lives, is very smart on the magnetic sea. We have to remember that successful, to my understanding, really means one that has achieved its mission or fulfilled its purpose. And this will cause great strife in people, especially the ones who do not understand their mission or purpose. These souls sit idle, waiting for something to tell them what their mission is, and yet no one can tell you your mission as much as you discover your mission and purpose. This bears repeating: <u>an individual must discover their purpose</u>. A free individual is one which wholly arms their ship, their mind.

A chained individual, endlessly waiting, is not in full control of their mind. For one reason or another they have relinquished controls and are not always making decisions. These kinds of people wait for decisions to be made for them. Unfortunately, I think that most of society is of the chained variety: Minds born of free will and relentlessly attacked by malicious intent.

The magnetic sea perhaps has many densities, rather than depths, and the different densities, or, currents, can enable the mind to travel at an efficient pace to its destination. It wouldn't be unreasonable to think then that in addition to a sea we may also discover oceans, rivers, streams and lakes, since even magnetism must flow in its own peculiar ways.

The ever-present flows of magnetism is necessary to maintain the health of the imaginary system. There will certainly be other presences in this new terrain, for example, hope and despair, and there will be many new surprises as our rational competencies develop. Certainly this isn't the place to fully map out the magnetic world that is hidden from our sight. But I only introduce it so as to better grasp what we are dealing with. By deciphering the greater territory, at least the existence of it, we find ourselves within a new context. This new context, is seems to me, is well-traveled and poorly understood.

Well, at least poorly understood by the mainstream and likely well understood by the mental elite, call them magicians or call them *mentalists*. But we must be certain these things I introduce here are not new things, rather they are things upon which the nature of reality works at the fundamental level.

This is essentially what we are working with since in order to claim full control of our hijacked free will we need to comprehend the details of this thing so often labelled as a prison of the mind. So now you see that there is no prison. There are no walls.

There is only terrain. There are ships and there are souls. And there is a notion called "free will" that by its very definition connotes freedom, that is, the central meaning of free will is a will that is free. A will that, by right, is owned by you; otherwise it would have just been called "will."

Thought Protection

How does free will fit into our imaginary world This is an interesting question, isn't it? We know that the captain represents our soul. We have come to understand that the five crew members represent the five emotions: anger, joy, worry, fear and grief, as well as their opposites. So in total we have ten (10) emotions and therefore ten (10) crew members.

We have learned that the propulsion system is an intention-based engine controlled by: congruency, compassion, confidence and conviction. We now understand that thought is the compass and therefore the directional system, call it navigation system if you will.

The mind which enables us to travel on the magnetic pathways is the ship and experience is the great voyage.

If all of this is true, to our best understanding, then what of free will? Free will is exactly what? Free will is a process that enables decision making. The decision making process necessarily entails the aspect of choice. So on the surface, we can conclude that choice is given to us because of free will. Yet that seems too simple, too simple because we have to remember that there are two variables in the dream making process known as fate and destiny.

Fate and destiny, at least for those who accept such notions, in many ways determine the choices we make, or, better said, determine the *important* choices we make.

Obviously, deciding on which bread is best is not an incredibly important choice. Deciding on what to study at university or who to marry are important choices. Well then, if we bring free will into this we can see we have the choice to marry who we want, and so often do without regard, but if we look deeper we will see, especially when looking back, that the person we chose to marry was necessary for us to gain a particular experience as part of our overall purpose. We can also say that no experience is a good or bad experience in its own way.

It is only an experience that we chose. Of course, we have to be reminded that our minds may have been maliciously hijacked at the time and this may have led to very poor decisions and what may be seen as bad fate, or, we may have made choices in line with our purpose and experienced a life of bliss. We can already see the important of owning a clear mind.

Before we fall too far off track let us examine once again the aspect of free will.

Thought Protection

Free will gives us choice and choice is influenced by fate and destiny, so revealing fate and density influence free will. But to say such a thing we mean to say that many of our voyages are replanted because if free will is influenced by fate and destiny then how much free will is there? Well, I'd have to say that there is not much free will to work with, but it exists the same by enabling the aspect of choice. Choice, in many ways, adds flavour to our journey.

And yet our voyage is largely planned, so we reach to the crux of an issue: can we have choice if the journey is determined? Well, that would depend on some very deep aspect that we need to look at, and that is the aspect of reincarnation. Why?

Well, obviously this journey belongs to you. You are the captain of your ship. It would only seem reasonable to say that you yourself planned this journey. What did he say? I said that you planned this journey. And if you did, you did so before you were incarnated. You plan the journey prior to making the journey. The journey is this life.

When we look at life this way we come to look at free will as this simple and often used word: faith. This is what I think that free will is. Faith is an unending sense that everything works out the way it was meant to work out, that is, the way you yourself meant it to work out. So faith can also be said to represent the connection between your mind and your soul. Your mind we have come to see as a ship; your soul as the captain, so faith is the connection between the captain and the ship.

I believe that this connection is best understood as ownership. You must recognize that you own this ship. Your mind is your mind. Let no one take that away from you. Let no one hijack or destroy your mind. Let no one cause you to lose this connection. No matter what happens keep the faith. Your mind belongs to you and you alone. So that is free will: ownership. The pink slip to your ship. The ownership papers. The ship is all yours captain. Where do you need to go now?

THE MEDIA PULPIT

It is unfortunate and abysmal and inconvenient that we have unwittingly, albeit willingly, traded the religious pulpit for a media pulpit. A *pulpit*, it should be noted, is a voice-box for ideological conditioning. All religion is steeped and constructed from ideological reasons using parables as a basis for teaching and learning.

What exactly is ideology? Ideology, if I would define it with my own sense of the word, is unwavering opinion founded upon fiction. Ideology serves a purpose. That purpose is to reprogram a mind; a human mind.

Ideology is everywhere, in every part of our collective thinking, in every facet of our modern world. Culture itself is based on survival because ethnicity is a very competitive vehicle and ethnic cleansing is a very consistent practice used over the course of history to concentrate power by eliminating the opponent.

The basis of the threat is opinion. You see, opinions form ideology and ideology threatens another ideology. This is why every culture, in fact every nation, must adhere to their own secular ideology, in order to protect their culture.

A culture, it should be noted, is founded upon the collective and historical ideology and formed into what is known as *religion*. And so we once again return to the concept of religion as the centerpiece of ideological thought.

All religions are based on sacred texts that are filled with the personal and metaphysical experiences of a spiritual individual. Some of these tomes are called meditations or gospels or books or scrolls or what have you. But if we look at the basis of any metaphysical writing, be it your own sacred journal, we will find the experience of an individual.

Over time, sacred texts accumulate and are compiled together and become singular books with lots of supplementary knowledge, but the single book is the sacred and public bible. So this is the situation of the bible.

Thought Protection

In any culture or religious faith – Judaism, Christianity, Buddhism, Islam – we will certainly find the appearance of one singular entity that is illuminated and all knowing. That all knowing entity is superior in every facet to a human being.

If we think about this situation of a superior enlightened being, a god, we begin to see that in order for society, followers, to accept the existence of a god, whether singular or plural, then those that are less superior, in descending order, are servants to that being.

So instantly we find ourselves with a hierarchical situation of worship. The less-enlightened worshipping the true being of enlightenment. The worshippers are inferior even though this is never explicitly stated. But it should be noted that the worshippers are superior to those the non-worshippers, the non-believers.

The believers worship the illuminated being and the non-believers are seen either lost or to be worshipping a dark entity, perhaps "Satan." In any and every organized religion, even in hybrid forms, we have the same scenario – the enlightened servants and the unconverted, the unworthy.

If we think about why this situation exists we immediately arrive at a simple, but non-obvious, truth and that is this: the presence of an enlightened being or all-knowing god demands subservience. The presence of that ultimate entity demands obedience and justifies any action to protect the truth, or word, or that ultimate entity.

In the name of religion all things can be accomplished and have been over the course of human history. But, you see, religion as a vehicle to demand obedience has largely transformed in a very subtle yet effective way. This is what is known today as *media*.

The word 'media' is an ancient religious place in Persia and Persia is the birthplace, the very core foundation of all religion. It is no coincidence that the media is now the ideological pulpit that we the people follow whether as knowing believers or unknowing non-believers. It does not matter your religious, or spiritual, preference because IDEOLOGY IS BEING SENT INTO YOUR MIND THROUGH ALL FORMS OF MEDIA.

Media has invaded every aspect of our lives whether it is the television, newspaper, magazine, book, radio or internet, and now, the rise of portable media players have only extended the ideological reach.

While it would be understandable that watching an entertainment program on prime-time TV would seem, on the surface, to be non-religious, if we think about this at a deeper level we would see that the creators of that program, whether knowingly or unknowingly, are spreading religious ideology. This is because both the producer and the actor share in similar ideologies and both of them share in the media corporation's ideology. The viewers in turn tend to agree with the show's ideology and ideology is founded upon religious belief; therefore, even an entertainment program on TV is spreading religious ideology.

You may be thinking at this point that there is nothing wrong with ideology or protecting a culture and to that I would agree. Yes, I said that I would agree with that.

Certainly human beings require a systemic way of thinking. They require an ideology; only the difference I would make between a constructive ideology or a deconstructive ideology is this: a constructive ideology does not tell a person what to believe, rather a constructive ideology only provides information, ideas and possibilities. A constructive ideology is never centered on a bible or set of secret texts because sacred texts infer ultimate truths and these ultimate truths don't exist. There is no ultimate truth, except your own ultimate truth. That truth is discovered in your own experience.

How and what you experience in this life is how and what you experience in this life. There is no ultimate truth; instead there is only personal truth. There is no singular bible there is a bible for every individual and this bible is in a continual process of being written. This is because as a human being filled with a spiritual body your ultimate purpose, assuming your missions and personal goals, is to remember who you truly are. Life is a purpose of discovery, to discover the things you already knew but forgot.

That is the unfortunate and abysmal and inconvenient state of the media pulpit. Not only is media steeped in religious ideology but also the media does not embrace constructive ideology and faithfully forms deconstructive ideology.

Deconstructive ideology is a form of ideology that tells you whether in direct or in subtle ways what and how to think. Constructive ideology enables you to think for yourself by providing you with all the tools.

So this is the current ideological environment in the world today. The basis of politics, military, banking and religion is founded on deconstructive ideology, and deconstructive ideology is an ancient form of ethnically competitive and cleansing thought.

Deconstructive ideology and its compulsory components such as mythological parables is the reason that malicious intent and negative intention came into practice. If you condemn improper intention behaviour, cast doubt into a person's thoughts or cause fear to spread then the followers are reminded why they have leaders. And when those leaders promise to eradicate evil and to chase away violence by providing criminals, whether real or invented, then the people's hearts and minds will been won over.

The path and practice of malicious intent is rampant across all nations. Every human mind, except those with a superior defence to such things, is infected to some degree. Even many of the leaders themselves are infected without knowing exactly where and to what extent. Certainly the purpose to infect a leader is to enable the spread to a larger population who cannot filter the varying levels of intention.

And so this is where we are, we are at an unstable period in human thought even though on the surface the modern society looks bright and cheerful. This will not last unfortunately; for the ultimate plan of malicious intent has yet to be revealed. The interim effect is control and a society living in a zombie-like fashion.

We are in effect a sleeping society. This concept is not new and has been debated many times before. Perhaps because now we are better understanding the technical configurations of this zombie system.

Malicious intent and negative intention are just modernized, even sanitized, versions of ethnic cleansing. Whereas the various inquisitions set about to murder or imprison those who did not agree with the Church, calling them *heretics*, today we have malicious intent as a way to cast doubt and fear into a human mind so as to subdue the mind and once subdued to suggest that everything will be okay if you obey.

And this is what any deconstructive ideological leadership wants – *obedience*. They do not want control because it is common to lose control of a mind; instead they want obedience because when you obey, as did Pavlov's dog, you are pain free. You see, rather than kill you or thrust you into a mental institution or prison they cause you immense pain, and, if you obey they give you great comfort.

Developed nations live in a life of comfort. We live in a house, drive nice cars, wear nice clothes, have nice friends and eat in abundance. This is also the reason for so much pollution and waste. But why would people care about pollution when they are so comfortable? They wouldn't. They don't care. The majority believe that they, as individuals, are important. To me the individual is not important. That is ego based thinking.

Malicious intent feeds the ego. It is easy to control people by feeding their ego and giving them comfort. This is also done using malicious intent.

Paris Tosen

THE MALICIOUS DETERMINATION

Before we explore malicious intent and its implications along with its treatment prospects, we invariably need to determine the specific parameters of maliciousness. We each have our own definition of *malicious*, and usually that definition includes the word "evil." This, unfortunately, is a misconception.

The concept of evil exists only within the context of good, that is, evil can only exist if good exists. That which is good is the reference point, in other words, if I said that a person or thing is evil then that also says that I am not evil, or, that I am good. Evil does not reference itself. Evil is always outside the reference point, and anything outside the reference point is never good.

So this is the predicament we are faced with. The reference point – be it a person, race, organization, or nations – is never evil, therefore it is good. Of

100

course the argumentative scholars and part-time religious followers trained in books and scriptures will argue, and rightly so, that good and evil exists. They will argue that a "god" implemented such things and they will have persuasive arguments supported by elegant and acute verse (translated usually). But those "scholars" will never ever believe that they are evil. In fact no one, as I've said, will label themselves as evil in a serious manner.

Those that may think that they are evil are delusional, as I will explain. But before that we have to understand that even a person who admits to being evil only does so to oppose a person who is labelled good; therefore the logic is the same.

The reference point is never evil, that is, the reference point is never wrong. And this is the key idea we have to understand. The idea or right and wrong.

Right and wrong, as with good and evil, do not exist. For right and wrong to exist we need to be divided, which we are, and, we need to maintain the idea of good and evil.
So what is there if there is no good and no evil? There is only choice. If you understand, and accept, that reality is an experiential construct, that is, a

stage of interaction, which it is; and if you accept the fact that you chose the blueprint of your life experiences, whether you are a suicide bomber or a nun, then you will understand that this experiential life only plays itself out and as it plays you reach certain pivotal points – nodes, junctures, crossroads – where you get to make a choice. You are destined to learn particular things but it's your choice in what circumstances those lessons are learned.

The idea of free will means that you are not bound to the experiences of your life. For example, rather than marry the person you love you can marry the person you don't love. You know the person you love, you know the person loves you and yet you marry another. Why would you do that? Free will.

We only cover these things in brief so as to better understand what it is to be malicious. Malicious is not evil because good and evil do not exist, these are man-made concepts and have been reinforced through education.

Right and wrong do not exist because good and evil do not exist, which is the basis of right and wrong. Choice exists and is utilize by the power of freewill.

If these concepts are true then what exactly is maliciousness? To comprehend maliciousness we have to comprehend the pseudo-science of electromagnetic energy. Although steeped in science, electromagnetism is really a part of metaphysics. They are in fact the same thing. Metaphysics is electromagnetism dealing with the living things, such as the human being.

Electromagnetic energy is dealing with science and technology, or, non-living things, such as artificial machines. But it needs to be understood that the metaphysical body interacts with electromagnetic energy in very profound ways.

Thought, for example, travels on electromagnetic energy. You see this in radio, for example, where a radio host's voice travels through air and is decoded by a radio and translated via a speaker to your ears. At the sample level, a radio, we have a metaphysical body interacting with an artificial machine.

Thought is translated into speech and speech is translated into a packet of energy and sent across using a particular electromagnetic frequency to reach a particular radio station, with its own unique address, or, frequency. All of these steps belong to the same process, and thought exists as a frequency. We can hear our own thoughts.

Usually we are unable to hear other's thoughts. But some people can hear other's thoughts. Some people, we must remember, can hear dead people speak, or can interact with spirit guides, or, can speak to god. We are always dealing with the same process.

What is the process? That process is the process of frequency modulation and demodulation. We've all heard of brain waves, right? We've all heard the comment that "we're not on the same wavelength." These things deal with frequencies; And there are a number of frequencies just like in a radio, for example.

It is in the context of frequencies that we can come to understand the concept of maliciousness because maliciousness exists as a particular frequency or range of frequencies. In order to be malicious one needs only to gain access to those frequencies.

You can gain access to those frequencies either by accident or by purpose. A malicious frequency is a lower level frequency if we look at the spectrum of electromagnetism within the parameters of a metaphysical human being. To be malicious one needs to access the lower frequency range. Higher frequency ranges enable communications with spirit beings, be it angels, star beings, or god. The label we use is regardless. The facts remain that more advanced, your higher self, more advanced beings, more spiritual things, that is higher frequency interplay, are on the upper end of the spectrum.

It is unfortunate that even science, because of its division with spirituality, isn't able to proves such things, but in time this will be done. So your thinking will be that of a pioneer since this knowledge isn't well known and even less understood.

A person who is considered to be **malicious in nature** has the following characteristic or attributes: lives in fear, worships ego, believes in greed, desires power, agrees with selfishness, wants wealth for the sake of wealth, concerned with self image and beauty, uses violence as a response or tool, addicted to control, unable to detach from material things, unable to love someone else, unaffected by other's opinions, feeds off the higher energies of others, infects others with their lower energies.

A malicious entity (be it a person, group, organization, corporation, government or nation) can be very detrimental to its environment and to the people around them. Because of the infectious nature of a malicious entity and the defenceless nature of normal, everyday people it is easy for a malicious entity to gain the upper hand.

Of course this is only the case because most people are unable to properly defend or shield themselves against maliciousness.

So you see, being malicious has nothing to do with being evil and everything to do with electromagnetic frequency.

Let it be made clear that anybody and everything can become malicious just as anybody and everything can become enlightened. These then are the two different ends to the Metaphysical Spectrum.

On one end we have **maliciousness** (previously referred to as evil) and on the other end we have **enlightenment** (previously referred to as good). From enlightenment, to maliciousness is the distribution of our world.

Thought Protection

Since a malicious entity craves these things such as control and power and wealth it is highly likely that a person or organization that has control and power and wealth has maliciousness, of course, this is not always true, but is usual. The more enlightened the entity, the less craving they have for these ego-based desires and the less attachments to material things. Enlightened people do not live in material abundance.

Look at your own life and see, perhaps, where you stand in the metaphysical spectrum. Do not be fooled by your ego which will lie to you in order to protect is material interests.

Remember that even a things such as beauty is self-referential, in other words, like good and evil, beauty doesn't exist. The selfish individual will tend to hoard beauty while the generous individual will tend to allow truth.

A person who is considered to be enlightened in nature has the following characteristics, or attributes: lives in courage, believes in nothing, understands nothing, desires truth, agrees with generosity, wants peace for the sake of compassion, concerned with the welfare of others, uses love as a response or tool, addicted to openness, unable to attach to material things, unable to hate someone else, affected by other's opinions, feeds others who may be low in energy, is able to raise the level of other's energies.

An enlightened entity (be it a person, group, organization, corporation, government, or nation) can be very beneficial to its environment and to the people around them. Because of the generous nature of an enlightened entity and the malicious environment within which they exist it is easy for an enlightened entity to become overburdened and burned out. Of course, this is only the case because most people do not understand how to manage their metaphysical selves, as well as, because the current level of civilization is flooded with malicious intent and it is nearly impossible to avoid it in the world. At this point and time, malicious intent is in control and is certainly suppressing society as a whole. The hypnotic state of a sleepwalking society is verifiable proof of this and this is why we must understand the combination of a metaphysical body coexisting in a field of electromagnetic energy.

The time now is insufficient to prove the validity of all the knowledge contained herein and that is why you must take it upon yourself to see the truth for what it is. The benefits to your life will be immeasurable. The benefits to the environment will be unquestionable. It is time to look at malicious intent.

THE METAPHYSICAL SPECTRUM

A woman naturally has a higher rate of vibration than a man. His is neither good nor bad. But in the old days of Church, the more spiritual woman had to be suppressed. Today, this is no longer the case because men and women can practice religion and, practice spirituality according to their own desires.

Only the centuries of spiritual suppression and, in the modern world, malicious intent, has led to deep ambivalence into the nature of our being.

Suppression has led to identifying confusion, and this confusion still serves our masters. We are reminded of the way (the) Buddha became enlightened was simply to sit under a tree and not move.

Thought Protection

A human being is ideally grounded in the community wavelength and has easy and regular access to the higher frequencies. The influenced society, such as the slumber society can have their collective frequencies, in this case lowered, in order for malicious entities to control the population. At the same time a society steeped, even swimming, in the lower wavelengths are living in comfort since that is the case for material things and wealth.

They are also living in surface beauty and apparent wealth but underneath the superficial layer of a nation the people are in deeper moral and spiritual pain. The ideal position it would seem would be to balance the material components with the immaterial truth, that is, since we exist as physical bodies we naturally must be rooted in the lower frequencies of a material body.

If we only existed at the higher frequencies we could not exist in the material world, we would transcend this platform of existence.

Spirit beings, including angels and star beings, do not have the same kind of material bodies as humans, and therefore exist, primarily, at the higher frequency. This is why we have difficulty with seeing them with our eyes or our cameras. The infrared spectrum is a higher frequency as are microwaves.

Can you see microwaves flowing in and around your food in a microwave oven? Microwaves are invisible to our naked eyes. Now imagine if a spirit being existed in the microwave range of electromagnetic energy. We obviously could not see it nor interact with the being since we are operating on different frequencies.

This is no different than having two radios tuned into two different stations. They would not interfere with each other. There are occasions where frequencies do cause interference, or feedback, and this is because they are sharing parts of the same frequency. For example, you may meet someone who makes you feel uncomfortable or confuses you or causes you to shift states, this is because there is a difference in each of your frequencies with certain similar parts.

If we look at the metaphysical spectrum of frequency modulation and demodulation we begin to get a sense that the nature of things exist as a frequency, or, more specifically as a *vibration*. The frequency of that vibration then is what determines the exact existence of a thing or group of things. If we play with that frequency of a vibration we can alter things or bring things into the play of things.

So this is the situation, we have human bodies as metaphysical beings, that is composed of a spiritual body and a flesh body, and these metaphysical bodies then interact within the complexities and construct of a vibration coded world.

Each human being has within itself a particular identity, commonly called a personality, and that identity is at a fixed address. By adjusting the parameters of human existences, that is, by adjusting the identity of the human being, by changing their address we can adjust or modify a society. But the more you move a human being away from their original address, their true selves, the more robotic, or, artificial and suggestive they become.

The situation at this time is such that the human beings have been deluded into a) changing their own address in pursuit of material wealth, or, b) been maliciously influenced to change, and/or remain in the lower frequencies of the metaphysical spectrum.

If you want to get back to a state of equilibrium, or, balanced life then you need to identify your true self, that is, to understand the characteristics of who you really are, in that way you will obtain your identity address and therefore can make progress to reach your true self.

The current barrage of malicious intent distracts human beings from understanding who they really are by telling them who they must be. This is an ancient case of idol worship. We create idols and then we make you convinced that you should be like those idols. The idols themselves are empty shells, they are malicious nothings designed to lure you into a life of material things.

The wealth of a nation then flows into the handful of elitists who control the population. The only way to stop this *loop-back* system is to cleanse yourself of maliciousness and then to protect yourself from further malicious intent and other negative intentions.

Only then will you see who you really are and only then will you be able to return to a state of equilibrium. And only then will you be able to gain regular and meaningful access to the wisdom of your spirit beings.

Thought Protection

It is in a way kind of like growing up in a household that has broadband internet and then slowly that broadband becomes smaller and smaller until your service is blocked. In your natural state, that is, what you are born with, you have broadband access that is unremovable, it is part of your metaphysical body.

The only way to stop that broadband access is to either block it or detour your services, or both. This is what malicious intent is capable of doing. Malicious intent does not want you to have broadband access to your true self. Why? Because then you will discover that you are already perfect and that spirit beings are your friends.

What does that mean to malicious entities? It means that they will lose control over you. This is called waking up. Waking up, you see, is still a choice. You still have, and always will have, free will. No one and nothing can remove free will, only you can elect not to choose. Malicious intent distracts you enough so that you will forget that choice was ever available.

But that choice is always available. Free will is an innate ability that cannot be removed. Now if you are infected with malicious intent and lead a very distracted life then you have unknowingly, and perhaps gladly, handed over free will to malicious entities.

The problem is that it is hard to know the exact state of affairs without removing all the malicious intent from your system. Only when the malicious intent is removed will you be able to understand your true self and your mission on this planet. It is hard to understand or remember things when you are sleepwalking. In fact, it is even difficult to understand things after you wake, that is, you cannot believe the things you did, as if it was in a dream. Life feels like a dream because of this situation of a slumber society.

Many readers of this book, the tough critics will react very strongly to the contents of this book. This is expected. There is an old adage that says the truth hurts.

This is the first time scientific concepts have been so blended with spiritual concepts, but I remind you that these things, these metaphysical things are part of your metaphysical bodies, spirit contained within the clothing of flesh.

The only learning that needs to be done is learning how to remember who we are since that is what we forgot as we became hypnotized. The more you wake from your unnatural slumber the more you will remember of who you are.

Who are you? You need to wake up to find out. To wake up you need to clear your mind. Clear your mind of malicious intent then you will wake up and then you will know who you really are.

WHAT IS MALINTENT?

Malicious intent is a general-term used for intention that alters certain beliefs such as lifestyle, choices, ideologies, or affecting your personal convictions, usually without asking your permission. You might have been affected by malicious intent or other altered thoughts on your mind if:

You are feeling depressed even when your life is good.

The goals you originally set (your life plan) or your goals you wish to set keep dragging even though you'd prefer different.

You catch yourself watching or reading certain news items that you don't find interesting, and find it difficult to busy your mind with other things.

Thought Protection

You mind has a hard time processing basic information, and you might experience regular headaches.

You experience a sudden overload of emotion or stress.

Malicious intent is often associated with intent that causes melancholy (called depression) or intention that multiplies stress or fear levels. That does not mean that all intention which causes melancholy or spreads fear is bad.

For example, you might ask a professional friend for their advice, but their advice may include some tough talk about their impressions of you. If you asked for someone's opinion of you and their intention is well placed the truth may still be hard to bear. You might also hire a therapist or trainer whose job it is to fix your outlined problems or to improve your performance.

Other kinds of unwanted intention will add so much negative information to your mind that can be stressful and can cause you to have anxiety attacks or experience a breakdown. These intentions have the ability to change your personal or professional goals, or force you to make irrational choices that are unsuitable to your personality and improvement with your way of thinking. These intentions also make it very difficult for you to go back to your original goals. These types of unwanted intentions are also often called Malicious Intent.

The key in all cases is whether or not you (or someone who makes decisions for you) understand what the intention is for and have agreed with their point of view and perspective.

There are a number of ways malicious intent or other unwanted intention can get into your mind. A common trick is to covertly download the intention during the download of either intention you enjoy such as a live news update or late night variety programs on TV. Whenever you are downloading across any media, make sure you carefully pay attention to the author's point of view, including their preferences and opinions. Sometimes the inclusion of unwanted intention in a given information acquisition is given as a warning, but it may not be clearly stated within the portion of information sharing or program viewing, rather may best be understood by the ideologies of the authors or the production company and its affiliates.

Signs of Malicious Intent

If our thoughts start to become negative or displays any of the symptoms listed below you may have malicious intent or other unwanted opinions downloaded into your mind.

Some unwanted, and negative, ideas will fill your thoughts that aren't part of your usual way of thinking. These ideas are often depressing and loaded with fearful scenarios you find overbearing. If you have deeply negative thoughts as soon as you open your eyes in the morning or when you're eyes in the morning or when you're out at a party, you may have malicious intent or other negative intention on your mind.

Some negative intention has the ability to change your goals or thinking process. This means that the goal you had yesterday or last week, perhaps even a task list, may be replaced with goals and tasks that you are not very familiar with or even uninspiring. Even if you rewrite down your goals, you may find that they revert back after a shorter period of time.

My media habits have become very different from what they used to be.

I feel melancholic all the time.

My thinking feels slow

Malicious intent and other negative intention are not necessarily designed to be productive and enlightening. The regions of the brain these thoughts use to alter your perception and decision-making process can severely slow down your thinking; and illogical or conflicting information can make you experience a kind of nervous breakdown.

If you notice a sudden increase in the number of times your thought processes are negative, or if your thinking is slower than normal at making routine decisions, you may have been infected by malicious intent or other negative intention on your mind.

If you realize that it is very possible that your mind is infected with malicious intent then you need to understand how to get rid of malicious intent.

HOW TO GET RID OF MALINTENT

Many kinds of negative intention, including malicious intent, are purposely sent for long-term confusion. If you try to rationalize through this intention like any other thought, you might find that the thought re-enters your mind not long after you thought you removed it.

If you're having trouble removing/ overcoming negative intention, you may need to spend some time in meditation to isolate the negativity and to rewrite over it with positive intention. Several forms of meditation are available either in book or workshop form and any of these can enable you to isolate negative beliefs and other malicious intent and help you to overcome it. *(I am unable to recommend any program of this sort.)*

To Remove Malicious Intent

1. Practice daily meditation.

2. Use the Meditative State in the Unconscious platform to isolate the negativity.

3. Review the ideas discovered through meditation for malicious intent and other negative intention.

4. Select suspicious thoughts for removal and erase them from your thinking process.

5. Research and study correct or positive information and rewrite over negative ideas.

6. Look for repeating patterns, detrimental ones, and isolate the root then practice to correct it through first understanding it.

7. Practice wrapping an invisible mindshield (firewall) around yourself and program it to filter out any malicious intent.

8. In meditation, for example, remove any unwanted or incompatible ideas or information by asking this data to be deleted or flushed out. Do this often.

9. Use diet and mental cleansing programs and reduce intake of artificial sweeteners and processed foods.

10. Spend time in nature or by the ocean; fresh mountain air.

Thought Protection

How to Prevent Malicious Intent

Malicious Intent and other negative intention can invade your state of mind, bombard you with melancholic ideas, slow down your decision-making process, and even make you susceptible to anxiety attacks and breakdown. Here are several ways you can help protect you mind against malicious intent and other negative intention.

Step 1: Use a neural firewall

Step 2: Clear your mind

Step 3: Adjust your info settings

Step 4: Learn and practice meditation

Step 5: Use media with caution

Step 1: Use a neural firewall

While most malicious intent and other negative intention are spread through the major media outlets or originate from unscrupulous vendors, a small amount of malicious intent can actually be placed on your mind remotely by polluted individuals.

Installing a neural firewall or using the logic firewall that's built into your mental software provides a helpful defence against these polluted individuals. To learn more about neural firewalls, read the Chapter on Neural Firewalls.

Step 2: Clear your mind

If your heart and mind are relatively healthy and balanced, one way to prevent malicious intent and other negative intention is to make sure that you clear your mind on a regular basis.

The process of clearing your mind also enables the metaphysical insights and energies of love to enter your mind.

How do you clear your mind? Find your own method, be it regular yoga practice, walks by the ocean, painting, choir singing or long drives on a mountainside, it's up to you to know. Stay away from prescription drugs, alcohol and heavy foods or other addictive habits like gambling.

Step 3: Adjust your info settings

You can adjust your mind's information acquisition settings to determine how much – or how little – information you are willing to accept from any single media source at a given time. I recommend that you set the information settings for the media to High.

To understand your current mental settings:

1. Think about your level of gullibility, your level of fatigue, time of day, etc.
2. Select the most relevant criteria according to the program you're watching or the article you're reading.

Your mental information settings for media are normally set according to your age, education, parental influence, disposition and level of interest in the program, ie a Christian will favorably watch a Christian program without much defence.

Step 4: Learn and Practice Meditation

Make it a daily ritual to access the Meditation Platform. Meditation is just one term of many, but essentially meditation is thinking within oneself for the purpose of exploring or reflecting upon oneself. Reflection, daydreaming, listening to your heart are all forms of meditation. The term is useful if it helps you; otherwise, make up your own term.

No matter what you choose, you should practice your deep, inner reflections, even taking notes, to better understand what should be a part of you and what needs to be removed.

Step 5: Use media with caution

The best defense against malicious intent and negative intention is not to make yourself a target in the first place. Here are a few helpful tips that can protect you from receiving intentions you don't want:

Only access media sources that are fair and balanced. If you're not sure whether it's fair and balanced, ask someone whose opinion you respect or search the web for reviews and reports critical of that show.

Access a variety of media, even ones considered controversial, in order to get a complete view of information and knowledge.

Never immediately agree or disagree with any new information. Instead, study, think and discuss with others before making a decision. Decisions are easy to make and hard to break.

Be wary of "popular" programs and movies, and be sure you understand that all of the ideas in those circumstances will have positive and negative thoughts and ideas so well mixed that it will be nearly impossible to separate fact from fiction. This is an easy way to confusion.

MORE WAYS TO REMOVE MALICIOUS INTENT

- meditation (reflection)
- study art (painting, sculpture)
- attend a live performance (theatre, music)
- take a vacation away from home
- go for a long walk outside
- spend time in nature
- swim in natural water or bask in sun or hike a mountain
- surround yourself with loving individuals
- spend time in isolation to read, listen to music, contemplate
- moderation in all things

- throw away things that are no longer useful (including relationships); detachment and forgiveness
- open yourself to love
- use prayer
- try to remember your dreams and to interpret their symbolic meaning
- accept truths about yourself
- get off religion, if possible

SYMPTOMS OF PROLONGED EXPOSURE TO MALICIOUS INTENT

- easily distracted, hard to focus
- feelings of anger or patterns of violence
- feelings of pervasive sadness or emotional outbreak
- inability to show affection or compassion
- reptilian mind, cold-blooded attitude
- addiction to substances, foods, or actions (eg sex, gambling, shopping)
- balance of craving, desires, needs and wants, ie having enough and being able to resist temptation is sign of a stable mind
- unable to trust people or situations
- unexpected mental illness onset
- psychotropics, or neuroleptics fail to treat conditions effectively

- math disorder
- reading disorder
- Social withdrawal, disinterest, fear, also signs of malicious intent present in your system
- Bipolarism (bipolar disorder)

Malicious intent alters the energy dynamic of the metaphysical mind and therefore enables these sorts of illnesses to possibly occur or increase.

As malicious intent is erased and released into the universal light and you clear your mind you will find yourself attuned to a different vibrational frequency, a cleaner and higher frequency.

You can be certain to experience new things and to look at life in a different manner. You may have new insights into the meaning of your life; you may even change certain parts of your life. As much as this may disorient you, the more you embrace those changes the more you accept the fact that you deserve those changes. You accept the fact that you are reading to change, and this is a very important element of your life.

Readiness precedes change and acceptance confirms your readiness. Embrace these ideas because you deserve the great gifts of life: love, joy and compassion. The rest is just stuff.

Extreme case of malicious intent and other negative intention in your human system has to do with mental instability, that is, loss of the mind, or, commonly, and poorly, defined as insanity.

What is insanity? Loss of mind, mindlessness. When you lose your mind and the further you lose your mind, you reach an area known as insanity, or, also called *mental illness* in the medical literature.

Mental illness is poorly understood and poorly defined, and, interestingly enough, mental illness is incurable. Rather than a cure, physicians, primarily psychologists and psychiatrists (alienists), work stringently toward treatment and management of the mind disease, knowing full well that a complete remission is outside of the control of the medical profession.

It is obvious that the complex nature of mental illness has been locked up within the confines of a limited thought process.

Thought Protection

That thought process is limited in a way that is strikingly similar to the limitations of excess malicious intent.

In other words, and in a very simplistic sense, there is an imbalance in the mind and its operations are not functioning properly.

JUSTIFICATIONS FOR MALINTENT

In order to be vigilant and complete we must understand the realms and possibilities for the presence of malicious intent. The whole idea of a mind, that of a human being, having being hijacked by unscrupulous people rests upon a very important precept.

What is that precept? There must be a valid, even if unreasonable, reason. Every thought and subsequent action requires a reason through that, or those, reason may be unknown or unclear for some time.

So why exactly have human minds collectively been hijacked? The first and most popular response would be control.

Thought Protection

Those unscrupulous, dark-minded individuals wish to control the plane and all of its inhabitants. Control also inevitably means money, wealth and that of a lavish lifestyle.

With power we gain access over all things and we set the standard as a kind would decree a rule to his people, as a priest would evangelize to his followers, as a singer to his fans. Power exists and has always existed, and it has always existed as both good and bad depending on who was in power.

It is obvious that there are elitists who hold power in this current reality and they decide much of the laws that we, as people, must follow. It is also obvious, maybe less so, that we the people far outnumber the elite rulers of our kingdom.

So that is the situation, the few managing the many simply because the many are indifferent to the specifics of their rule. That indifference of course is due to the fact that our minds have been hijacked, and therefore we are not in a decision-making mode.

I do feel that these elitists – secret societies, cabalists, illuminati, cultists – do desire control. But I feel that control is but one part of the process to their diabolical goals. Control is necessary as a first step. You see, control enables these elitists, all them cultists for sake of identification, to enact their larger plan, and when a larger plan exists that larger plan then becomes an agenda.

They begin with the accumulation of wealth in an economic world and that wealth then leads to positions of power. Positions of power, although not completely unchecked, allows the accumulation of widespread control. But what is the real purpose to their agenda?

Control, it would seem on the surface, is relatively easily achieved and not a very lofty goal. I mean, control is meaningless and unimaginable over the long-term, unless it is a means to an end. For example, one does not go through university to obtain a Master's Degree. One obtains a Master's Degree to secure a well-paying, high-level position that garners lots of respect and jealousy.

You could say that a person with a Master's Degree has obtained a certain amount of power, and that power is used to gain a position of control. But does it stop there? The accumulation of control and power and wealth, when handed over to individuals based in ego (ie sociopaths), ultimately enables them to do something very relevant to our discussion – enables unprecedented action. Control is permission to control the outcome. That is the purpose of control. It is not to end in control, rather all things begin in control. So you see these cultists in control, armed with wealth and power, are determined to take unprecedented action. An action of the likes we haven't seen in many years and lifetimes.

Let's review the Cult Agenda briefly: elitists with power and wealth who belong to some kind of interconnected secret society. Many of them hold positions of power, whether public or private, and many of those are aged, well aged. These cultists influence and initiate all manner of war because they have command and influence to the military.

These cultists are wealthy beyond measure because they either own outright, or, in majority, the key global banking institutions. The Cultists control major religions. So what do we have so far? Cultists either own, influence, or control the four pillars of society: politics, military, banking and religion. These four pillars of society is the umbrella under which we live our lives.

In politics, we can also include law, and this first pillar dictates how a society is ruled and how it is punished for disobeying those rules. The idea of democracy is far superior to outright fascism because democracy, on the surface, is for and by the people.

In practice this is not true. Democracy is for and by the rulers; for the rulers, be if the President or the Judge, shape what is best for the people. The people do not write the laws, the politicians do. The lawyers only follow the laws for their own purpose.

This is why a mass murderer may escape prison sentence and why a mad father who kills his wife is jailed for life.

Laws are not written for the purpose of fairness. In fact, laws are written for the purpose of arbitrary control. If you have the clout, the money and the skill you can escape any charge, but if you have political enemies, few funds and an appointed defence attorney you will be locked away for a very long time, regardless of your crime.

The military also includes technology and science since most technology is first explored and deployed on the battlefield because there is always a need for more intelligent technology. If there were no wars there would be no reason to develop tactical weaponry or communications technology.

It is not the purpose here to look at the depths of military technology or the history of war and its casualties. We are only trying to understand some of the reasons, or singular reason, why the Cult uses malicious intent on it unsuspecting population. (Of course our most convincing proof is a terribly destabilized, unbalanced and violent world of which was influenced by our rulers, our representatives.)

If there are military objectives then it would seem like a reasonable motivation. Military and politics are fed by large sums of money. This is why the third pillar, banking, is necessary. Banking is a way to keep society, hardworking members of the public, in debt.

Debt is a very effective way to suppress ideological warfare against the Cult because citizens are too preoccupied with paying their monthly mortgage, because if they fail to Pay, the home will be repossessed.

And then we come to religion. Religion is a form of control through fiction. Religion is an outlet for myth sharing. The problem is that people, worshippers, believe those collective myths are truth when in fact those myths are fictional parables not literary fact.

All religious tales are parables that have been passed down for thousands of years as if you took a story like Peter Pan and photocopied it for the next ten thousand (10,000) years.

Of course, the idea of Peter Pan today and ten thousand years from today would be really different even though the story of Peter Pan is basically the same. Now, imagine that the star of Peter Pan goes through various edits and reinterpretations (reimaginings), wouldn't that change the details of Peter Pan?

It is the story of the fisherman who catches a fish and after telling ten people the story becomes distorted because it is in the nature of mankind to interpret for their own purposes, according to the size of their ego.

They do not interpret according to truth, but according to ideology.

Thought Protection

Man is a very ideological creature. They will create ideology in order to agree with their beliefs, in order to fit the size of their ego. Isn't this why we believe in gods?

So this then is what is ideology manifested in form – religion. The culmination of ideological, and dogmatic, belief is the formation of religion, and the construction of the temple, or church.

The original intent of religion was not to suppress thought but religion is power and power with ego leads to ideological suppression in order to maintain basis of and for power.

Whereas the pulpit of an evangelical conduit used to suffice, today the greatest preacher is media.

This is the purpose of media – to transmit ideological belief to the followers, only the followers known as viewers do not know that they are being fed an ideology. They instead feel that they are being entertained through cultural programming.

You see the problem now, entertainment has been filled with ideology, and ideology, once we break it down, is loaded with ingredients that are designed to deconstruct your thought process and to hijack your mental ship without your knowledge.

We have come this far and still we have not reached the real reason for this malicious intent. We now understand that there are forces at play against us and that our thoughts and minds are not completely at our command. But the big question, if not for power, is why? Why the control? Why the manipulation? Why hijack our ships? The 9/11 hijackers had a reason, of course they were not alone with their cult friends. Their goal was not even to destroy the twin towers. The goal; reason, for 9:11 was to further hijack the mind of the public.

Some of the reasons for control is to eliminate the competition. Who is the competition? The lightworkers and starkind. The competition wants peace and spiritual understanding in the Age of Aquarius. The Cult needs spiritual suppression to keep their power, and that act is getting more and more challenging as more and more people wake from their slumber.

USING A NEURAL FIREWALL

Interacting with any media without a firewall is like walking outside in your underwear. Although you may enjoy some of the fresh air, the weather elements will soon enough get the best of you.

In any media, ideological *spreaders* use malicious thoughts – such as outrageous ideas, words, and beliefs – to try to reach into unprotected minds. A neural firewall can help protect your mind against these and other personal/ viewpoint/ opinion attacks.

The need for protection against malicious intent is not only to defend against the strength of a negativistic word (eg infidel) or a deliberately confused phrase (eg war in the name of freedom), but, more importantly, and if not clear from all previous chapters, thoughts are energy and words are carriers of this energy. Think of malicious energy as malicious computer code that if it infects your system (mind) then it wreaks havoc. So, we require firewalls to filter and block out these energies (carried by words) that can harm our existential functions at the root of our being.

So what can a malicious spreader do? It depends on the nature of the mental attack. While some attacks are just conflicting information that may cause confusion, other are sent with dark purpose. The more challenging communications may attempt to cause memory loss, inspire hatred, or garner your support for an unfavourable cause, be it a product or political campaign.

Some spreaders even work to spread disinformation, or, information loaded with fact and fiction that makes it hard to separate the truth, like any good novel. Outrageous ideas, words and beliefs are destructive to mental health, for example, "We must give everything to protect our nation from attack." What does that mean? Is someone attacking the nation? What is the definition of an attack? How much is "everything"?

A statement like this instils paranoia because it basically says, if anything happens that is seen as an attack on our nation, as defined by us who said it, then you have to give everything we ask of you without question. Now, if this nation is a democratic, developed nation then obviously there is conflict with its freedom principles. Should it be required, anything can be construed to be seen as an attack, for example, discovery of anthrax in some unmarked envelope in some office somewhere could be used to show how some "terrorist" is after "us."

A malicious spreader can spread this code into a population enough times and the people, you, will feel like you are living in fear of some aggressors, regardless of whether anyone ever shows up. This allows the leadership to then install security systems, new procedures and the like all with your fearful willingness. You can use a mental firewall to reduce the risk of infection, and remain aware that something is not right.

How do I choose a firewall?

A mental firewall works by examining information coming from and going to your mind. It identifies and ignores information that comes from a dangerous (questionable) source or seems suspicious.

If you set up your mental firewall properly, spreaders sending negative information and data can't pierce your memory system, therefore the information is rejected, ignored or blocked, according to your specifications.

At the same time, you are aware of what was spread and the information it contained without having the adverse effects.

There are three basic types of mental firewalls that can be implemented. The first step in implementing a mental firewall is to determine which one is best suited to your personality and temperament. Your options include:

logic firewalls
knowledge firewalls
esoteric firewalls
disease firewalls

Thought Protection

To get started, answer these questions and record your answers:

1. How much interaction do you have with all media forms?
2. What is your intellectual and emotional aptitude at this current time? (This might be your own analysis or may be taken from some kind of examination.)

That's it. You are now ready to start thinking about what type of firewall you would like to use. There are several options, each with its own pros and cons.

Logic firewalls

Logic firewalls are a good choice for most people, and they work well regardless of your career or lifestyle. (scholars and mystics have a built-in logic firewall, perhaps an esoteric one may be of use.)

Logic firewalls can help you to see truth from fiction from a person. This is quite useful in family and work situations. For example, the boyfriend who can't answer some basic questions as to where he disappeared to for several hours the previous night might be in for some trouble if the woman applies the right filters and doesn't believe his lies.

Logic firewalls can see the discrepancy between different pieces of information and then will refuse or accept that body of information based upon its scan.

As an example, a government who states that they will spend all efforts to cure cancer and then billions of dollars later show an increase in cancer rates is an error in logic; for if they had invested wisely those billions they should have at least reduced cancer.

The next time the government makes any statement of this level you should not believe them so easily.

The other great logic example has to with star visitors (ETs) because the government and military deny their existence, but then have mounds of UFO files (that cannot be explained), then they say that if star visitors are real, then they are evil, well, if they don't exist and you've never seen them, how do you know if they are evil or not evil? Put up the logic firewalls.

Knowledge firewalls

The knowledge firewall is helpful for learning, especially when it comes to historical knowledge. History is a very subjective endeavour and can be changed easily by the roll of a pen.

Thought Protection

A knowledge firewall can help you sift through a body of knowledge, or books for example, to get to the truth, that is, even though 98% of all books say the same thing you might continue searching and find the 2% that say otherwise. If you easily accepted the first 98 books then you might never get to the truth. A firewall can help you continue and find the truth.

Esoteric firewalls

If you are intuitive, psychic or are planning to develop your spiritual abilities, you will need an esoteric firewall. Only a few mystical practices have a built-in firewall, so you may need to develop the following system.

The truth be told, when you enter the spiritual or esoteric field, you are entering a new dimension of existence and will be feeling a new batch of energies. This is like swimming in the Atlantic Ocean for the first time and there are unfriendly fishes that may come for you, not to mention the huge waves or cold water.

An esoteric firewall, a *mindshield*, can protect you from unwanted attacks as you now start picking up the negative energies of the masses, or the hate of a woman scorned. The esoteric field is quite complex (and mysterious) and if you are a sensitive type, or newly awakened, your best bet is to maintain a protective firewall around your mind at all times until you can tell truth from fiction, myth from magic.

Disease firewalls

Disease Firewalls are ideal when someone is susceptible to illness and also is afraid of disease in general. A disease firewall may be specifically necessary when a logic firewall may be insufficient.

The immune system is intimately connected to your state of mind; therefore, a clean state of mind ensures a clean immune system. The thought of disease, if it takes root into your pattern of thinking, becomes disease. Likewise, the thought of health or happiness becomes health and happiness.

Malicious intent can significantly lower your defense against thoughts about disease or the prevalence of certain strains of illness, such as a particular flu, and this will also likely cause your immune system to weaken and disease to enter. By the same token it may be the case that, for whatever reason, you yourself have a need to get sick and that desire becomes thought and that thought becomes sickness. For example, if you hate your job you may cause sickness in your body to miss out at work.

Disbelief is not enough to overcome the continual bombardment of malicious intent loaded with fear-based thought strains. In fact, disbelief in a perfect tool that fools your brain into thinking that you are not affected when in fact the other levels of fear tactics have by-passed your defences and entangled themselves in your pattern of thinking. These may not activate until other components are installed onto your mind.

These kinds of attacks are known as neural portals since they effectively create a portal into your neurological core and these portals attack negative intent from any other source that then enters your pattern of thinking without problem. In fact, by the time you realize that your thinking is substandard and negative, your mind may be infected with malicious intent and negative intentions deliberately designed to interfere with mental operation, memory, confusion, or depression, or spread themselves to other minds and throughout social network, often slowing things down and causing deep ambivalence in the process.

The birth of the mind-virus

Just as malicious intent range in severity from lies to brainwashing, mind-viruses range from mildly annoying to downright depressing, and come in new and different forms. The good news is that with a stable defensive mechanism in the process, and a little maintenance you are less likely to fall victim to mood swings and you can better manage your emotional states.

How do mind-viruses work?

Basic **mind-viruses** typically require unwary biological minds to inadvertently share or send them. Some mind-viruses that are more sophisticated, such as *spellware*, can replicate and send themselves automatically to other persons by controlling other thought processes, such as an emotional sharing. Certain *spellware*, called *schizoids* (named after schizophrenia), can falsely appear as a beneficial idea to coax your mind into accepting them. Some schizoids can even provide proven knowledge while quietly damaging your mental system or friendship circles at the same time.

Although it's good to be aware of these different types of mind-viruses and how they work, what is most important is that you keep your mind clear, stay aware of recent negative ideas, and ensure you practice a well intentioned lifestyle. Once a mind-virus is on your mind, its type or the method it used to get there is not as critical as removing it and preventing further infection.

How do I know if infected?

After a period of time of downloading negativity and fear onto your mind, you might not realize that you've introduced a mind-virus until you notice your behaviour isn't normal.

Here are a few primary indications that your mind might be infected:

- Decision-making process is slowed
- Withdrawn or absent-minded
- Skills and knowledge is out of sync
- Unable to listen or understand other people
- Speech isn't clear or doesn't make sense
- Change mind every half-hour
- You think everyone is against you
- You see yourself in a distorted or exaggerated way

- Make instant decision and then fail to follow through
- You think you are dying or about to die
- You completely trust or completely distrust a person or group

These are common signs of infection – but they could also indicate serious imbalance or disease in your body or mind or the fact that you are overworked and stressed from lack of rest, and this could have nothing to do with mind-virus. The bottom line is that unless you use anti-mind-virus intention in your mind, there is no way to be certain if your mind has been infected with a mind-virus or not.

Removing a mind-virus from your mind is a difficult task – without the help of specific tools designed to do the job. Some mind-viruses and negative intention are even designed to reinstall themselves after they have been discovered and cleared out. These kinds of malicious thought code are prepared by competent individuals and are less rare than you would imagine.

Although malicious intent is different from a mind-virus, some behave alike and pose similar or other risks.

Thought Protection

A neural firewall, in today's technological world, is a basic requirement. The terrain will be a little unfamiliar for most people while others do so automatically, but as more and more people search for the truth, more and more malicious intent will be revealed, and the more imperative it will be to learn about how to properly protect your human thought.

If you gained anything from this book then it is hoped that you are now more aware that the multiplatfrom world is real, despite evidence otherwise, and that thought defines and shapes existence, that is, to reconfigure your life, and life on earth, you need to pay particular attention to thought, and everyone's thought, and to not let misguided leaders take you to dangerous waters.

Be the captain. Protect your ship. And always know where you are going by using your compass.

What I did explain in the contents of this book certainly caused you to think and rethink as to the validity of such information. This was expected and normal so it was written with this anticipation in purpose, but I will remind the reader that it was certainly up to you to decide whether you would adopt this knowledge and to what degree. That is the beauty of knowledge in general terms: it is available to your criticism or acceptance.

Your choice of direction – criticism or acceptance – is a reflection of how you see the world, verily a reflection as to how you think, and that is worth thinking more about. Be thoughtful.

www.ingramcontent.com/pod-product-compliance
Lightning Source LLC
Chambersburg PA
CBHW060310290526
45789CB00001B/467